THE SCOUT'S BACKPACKING COOKBOOK

TIM AND CHRISTINE CONNERS

FALCON GUIDES

GUILFORD, CONNECTICUT
HELENA, MONTANA

AN IMPRINT OF GLOBE PEQUOT PRESS

FALCONGUIDES®

FalconGuides is an imprint of Globe Pequot Press.

Falcon, FalconGuides, and Outfit Your Mind are registered trademarks of
Morris Book Publishing, LLC.

Text design: Maggie Peterson
Project editor: Julie Marsh
Layout: Mary Ballachino

Library of Congress Cataloging-in-Publication Data is available on file.

ISBN 978-0-7627-7910-9

Printed in the United States of America

10 9 8 7 6 5 4 3 2 1

CONTENTS

DEDICATION

To the staff at Philmont Scout Ranch in the Rocky Mountains of New Mexico. Because of your commitment and hard work, many thousands of our Scouts have had the opportunity to walk among the life-changing beauty of our country's high places.

BENEDICTION

May the Lord bless his land . . . with the choicest gifts of the ancient mountains and the fruitfulness of the everlasting hills; with the best gifts of the earth and its fullness.

—Deuteronomy 33:13–16 (NIV)

ACKNOWLEDGMENTS

To the many Scout leaders from across the country who once again answered our call for recipes, tips, and suggestions, you have our heartfelt gratitude. The trail is the pinnacle of the Scouting experience, and you've helped fuel the journey. We'd like to especially recognize the talents and contributions of Scouters Curt White, Ken Harbison, and Sherry Bennett, each of whom was instrumental in building a solid foundation of recipes for this book.

Scott Daniels, now the former managing editor for *Scouting* magazine, cleared the trail one final time. Max Phelps, director of outdoor sales at Globe Pequot Press, sold the idea. And Jessica Haberman, acquisitions editor at GPP, made it real. Especially to you three, thank you.

To Gerred Bell and Ken Harbison, who assisted with recipe testing, you have our sincere appreciation. And special thanks go to our cadre of outstanding trail photographers: Ted Ayers, Max Coles, Mary Hibbard, Wayne Kodama, David Lattner, Jim Rausch, Scott Simerly, Robert Wagner, and Curt White.

Introduction

For the Scout accustomed to camping with gear hauled by the troop's utility trailer, the first backpacking trip can come as quite a shock. There are so many differences between trail and traditional camping, it sometimes seems the only thing the two have in common is the open sky above. The surprises are numerous, not the least of which is meal planning and preparation for the trail. It's always a good chuckle when an inexperienced Scout asks who is going to carry the cast-iron Dutch oven on the upcoming backpacking trip.

A pack stove and pot compared to a Dutch oven: Which would you rather carry on the trail? TIM CONNERS

A Troop Committee Member relayed the story of his encounter with the mindset of a new backpacker:

> *We spent three meetings covering what each Scout needed to carry on an upcoming ten-day trip. We even practiced preparing a few meals so they could sample powdered eggs and freeze-dried food before hitting the trail. When the day of departure arrived, we were running late and opted not to perform our usual pack inspection. After arriving at the trailhead, we shouldered our backpacks and headed out. Lunch was peanut butter and jelly supplied by the senior patrol, along with some partly thawed fruit drinks. Then it was off to our first campsite, arriving just prior to sunset. After a quick camp setup, the boys were told to prepare their dinners.*
>
> *One of the new Scouts soon came over and asked where the microwave oven was. We explained that there was no micro-*

wave oven on a backpacking trip. He then wanted to know how he was supposed to cook the frozen pizza he had brought. A panicked survey of the contents of his backpack soon revealed not one, but over twenty pizzas, plus twelve boxes of corn pops and a frozen quart of milk. Well, we had a lot of pizza that night, and everyone learned how to share their food for the remainder of the trip. When he made Eagle years later, we surprised the Scout with . . . dozens of frozen pizzas.

Our Scout from the example above may have missed some of the key points from his leaders' instruction, but explaining the nuances of backpacking to those new to it is normally fulfilling and a lot of fun. To the inexperienced, nearly all aspects of the activity seem almost magically impossible: lightweight and compact gear that nevertheless keeps one comfortable, warm, and dry. Food and cooking equipment that pack down into a small bag yet are adequate to feed a Scout for a week.

Scouters packing it in along the Blue Ridge.
TIM CONNERS

It isn't hard to understand why a novice might think this way when a typical trip to Scout camp can result in hundreds of pounds of gear per person loaded into the troop trailer. But to keep the weight of the backpack within a reasonable range, the gear and techniques used on the trail must be radically different than those used in camp. Despite the differences, however, cooking on the trail is like camp cooking in that once a few basic skills are acquired, it isn't difficult. And trail cooking doesn't require elaborate gear. With a decent stove and a few simple utensils, you can eat like a king.

While trail cooking doesn't have to be a major challenge, the strenuous physical nature of backpacking often is. Some trails would be difficult even without carrying a load. Add a pack, and the required exertion level rises dramatically. Compounding the problem is the need to keep the pack weight under a maximum reasonable limit, which can be a real strain on the skill of a novice backpacker.

It's always tough to resist the urge to carry many nonessential creature comforts that, collectively, can be very heavy. Especially on long trips, it is particularly difficult to avoid packing too much food, perhaps because of the common deep-rooted fear of going hungry far from town or home. It can take years of experience before a backpacker finally learns to avoid overloading his pack. Wise trail menu planning and preparation are two of the most important keys to assuring a manageable pack weight. These become more critical as the trip's duration increases.

Troop 340 prepares dinner on the AT. CHRISTINE CONNERS

Cooking on the trail is a unique problem requiring creative solutions. If you're new to the trail, this book addresses the skills necessary to meet the challenge by showing how to successfully plan and prepare a backpacking menu while keeping the weight of your food and cooking gear within reason. And whether expert or novice, over one hundred outstanding recipes spanning a wide range of preparation techniques and meal categories provide plenty of easy options for your next adventure.

The backcountry beckons and the high mountains call. As you follow the lure of the trail, may this book enhance the fun and fellowship that you and your troop or crew find in the wild places of the world.

USING THIS BOOK TO PLAN AND PREPARE YOUR MEALS

Ideal Attributes of Backpacking Food

A menu suitable for a backpacking trip is far different from one for the typical Scout camping event. With the load of food and cooking gear all on your back, combined with the lack of refrigeration, the nature of the game changes completely. A new set of attributes becomes most important when selecting and preparing your food for the trail, the criticality of each depending on the length of the trip and the conditions expected.

Weight of food and gear is always an important consideration, but it's more important as the length of your trip increases. For an overnight, for instance, canned goods, frozen meats, and fresh fruits and vegetables are possible options, though they're heavy for their nutritional value. On longer trips, as your pack load grows, an increasing fraction of dried food must be included because of its lighter weight for the same nutritional content.

Durability ranks high in importance with weight. Many are the horror stories of those who've attempted to bring fresh eggs or soft loaves of bread on the trail, only to discover that fragile foods don't fare well in the rugged environment found inside one's pack. Well-packaged dried and dehydrated foods, tough-crust breads such as bagels, hard cheeses and salami, and vegetable oils sealed in containers are all examples of durable foods that pack well and resist spoilage. But less-durable foods can also be acceptable for the trail, especially if the trip is of short duration and the weather not too warm.

Simplicity becomes very important to your menu on longer trips. While there is a time and place for a feast in the wilderness, trail life is usually challenging enough without difficult, multicourse meals. By primarily choosing one-pot meals and easier recipes, you'll carry less gear and fuel, and spend more time relaxing and less time cooking and cleaning.

Nutritional Value, Taste, and Variety are the remaining three key meal-planning attributes. These are closely related in the sense that they can be difficult to balance. New backpackers tend to select comfort foods that taste good but are poor in balanced nutrition. It's also a common mistake to pack a lot of the same type of food. Again, on a trip of short duration, nearly any menu will suffice, no matter how lousy, since the trailhead—and restaurants—aren't far away. But on challenging trips spanning more than a couple of days, quality nutrition becomes paramount for keeping your body operating at peak performance. Also, appetizing food, and a variety of it, become increasingly important for maintaining your interest in eating what's in your pack. Don't underestimate this point. The mental demands on the trail can be incredibly challenging; if all you've brought are lentils and oatmeal, it won't be long before you're desperate to get off the trail and into your favorite pizza parlor.

A sampling of trail-ready foods that are lightweight, durable, simple, nutritious, and tasty. *TIM CONNERS*

The recipes in this book take into consideration all of the above attributes and provide a variety of tasty options for any trail adventure, from overnight trips to excursions lasting a week or more. The recipes have been arranged to maximize the efficiency of the meal-planning process. Information is plainly presented to allow the reader to quickly judge the merits of a particular recipe while preparing for a backpacking trip. Each recipe is clearly and logically structured for foolproof preparation once on the trail.

The following sections of this chapter explain the general layout of this cookbook and how the information included can specifically assist with trail meal planning and preparation for your troop or crew.

Recipe Categories

Categorizing recipes is not as easy as it might seem. There are as many ways to organize a cookbook as there are eating styles and preferences. The approach that appears to satisfy most people, and the one used in this book, is to begin by organizing entrees according to the meal category that they best belong to: breakfast, lunch, or dinner. Those recipes that could not be tagged as "main dish" were grouped into three other primary categories: breads, snacks and desserts, and drinks.

The lunch section was constructed around the premise that noontime meals on the trail are primarily "no-cook." It is time-consuming to break out the stove, heat the food, then clean the gear after eating. This process is often better reserved for mornings at camp or later in the day, once you've arrived at your destination. In fact, it is not uncommon for backpackers to simply snack on a variety of healthy foods continually throughout the day while walking, with no real differentiation between "lunch" and any other break. Adapt these recipes according to the hiking preferences of your troop or crew.

Servings and Weights

Many recipes in this book, especially lunch and snack items, require preparation only at home. These recipes generally make a large number of servings, adequate for several Patrols or an entire troop or crew. The servings can be portioned and divided as required for each backpacker.

The story is different for recipes with final preparation steps performed on the trail. In these cases, the range in number of servings usually runs from one to no more than about six. Because of practical limitations on the size of gear that can be packed, the standard backpacking cook pot is generally not larger than 2½-quart capacity; six servings is about the most that can be expected from such cookware.

It may seem odd at first that many of the recipes are constructed for a single serving. There is good reason for this, the intent being that they'll be replicated as required to precisely meet the needs of your particular group size. These recipes are handy not only for this reason but also for permitting the tailoring of each individual's menu for their own unique preferences. One beauty of backpacking recipes is that they tend to be readily scalable in the number of servings, either up or down. Get in the habit of scaling as required; otherwise, you could find yourself either short on food or, often just as frustrating, carrying far too much.

For consistency, serving estimates assume the target audience to be active teenagers on a moderate caloric intake. Serving sizes were adjusted upward as credit for healthier recipes and downward for those with less desirable nutrition characteristics. Adjust your estimates according to your specific situation, keeping in mind that activity level, richness of the meal, food preferences, snacking, weather, and altitude will all influence the actual number of servings you'll obtain from each recipe.

For estimating the total weight of your packed food, the dried weight per serving is also included for each recipe.

Challenge Level

A three-tier system has been used to assign a challenge level to each recipe: "easy," "moderate," or "difficult." The decision was based on the preparation and cleanup effort required, the sensitivity of the cooking technique to variation, and the attention to care necessary to avoid injury. Most of the recipes in this book have been tagged as "easy," an important quality especially for the trail setting, where simplicity is definitely welcome. Because cooking on the trail is challenging enough, recipes considered "difficult" were purposely minimized.

Preparation Time

Total preparation time on the trail under pleasant weather conditions has been estimated for each recipe. This value includes time from lighting the flame through to serving the dish. It is assumed that the cook will flow the preparation steps in parallel whenever possible. For instance, while water is being brought to a boil, other preparation tasks can often be accomplished simultaneously. The recipes are written to best take advantage of this.

Preparation Instructions

Each recipe includes a list of ingredients and step-by-step directions, each logically grouped and presented in numerical sequence. The use of numerical sequencing is intended to help the chef stay focused and to assist in the assignment of specific tasks to other Scouts and Scouters.

All of the recipes require at least some preparation steps to be performed at home. These are clearly distinguished from final preparation steps required on the trail. *Be sure to bring along a summary of the on-trail cooking instructions for any recipes used on your trip so you won't be caught by surprise when it comes time to cook.*

Hot chili on a chilly evening. *DAVID LATTNER*

Options and Tips

Interesting cooking options are provided for many of the recipes. Options differ from the main instructions and produce alternate endings to the recipe. Options included with a recipe are shown separately from the main preparation steps.

Likewise, contributors occasionally offered helpful tips that assist the trail cook with purchasing ingredients or preparing the recipe. As with options, tips are listed separately from the main body of the recipe. Recommendations and tips of a more generic nature, or applicable to a wider range of recipes and situations, are presented separately in the following sections.

Equipment Requirements

A single cook kit of reasonable size can be expected to service as many as six people, but should be multiplied as required for larger groups. Not only does it make sense to do so from the standpoint of having replacement equipment when critical gear breaks on the trail, but it also prevents mealtime from turning into a long, drawn-out ordeal as Scouts would otherwise have to wait their turn to cook. Gear for the group's cook kit can be divided among the Scouts and Scouters for carrying on the trail.

Gear assumed to be essential equipment in a troop or crew's group trail cooking kit includes the following:

- Backpacking stove with windscreen and adequate fuel for the trip
- Small maintenance kit, appropriate for the stove
- Lightweight cook pot with stowable handle
- Cook pot lid that can double as a frying pan
- Short wooden or plastic stirring/serving spoon or ladle
- Short plastic spatula (if foods requiring frying are on the menu)
- Liquid measuring device (many water bottles have measurement scales)
- Ignition device, such as lighter, and waterproof backup ignition source
- Small container of hand sanitizer
- Small container of biodegradable detergent
- Small scrub pad and camp cloth
- Mesh bags for storing and airing food kit items

In addition, each member of the group should carry their own personal mess gear, including:

- Small, durable serving plate
- Durable, heat-proof drinking cup
- Lightweight spoon, fork, and knife, or spork (i.e., utensil combo)
- Filled water bottles for cooking
- Mesh bag for storing personal food kit items

An array of typical cooking gear for the trail.
CHRISTINE CONNERS

If a recipe's equipment needs go beyond the essentials noted here, those additional requirements have been listed below the preparation steps to head off any mealtime surprises on the trail.

Contributor Information

Rounding out each recipe, you'll find information about the contributors. These are the field experts, the Scout leaders who made the book possible. You'll learn their names, scouting title, place of residence, and the troop, crew, or pack and council they call home. Many contributors included anecdotes and stories to accompany their recipes. Useful and often humorous, you'll find these under the title.

Category System

This book uses a category system to allow the cook to rapidly assess the most appropriate recipe options when planning a menu for the trail. The six key attributes for backpacking recipes were discussed earlier: weight, durability, simplicity, nutritional value, taste, and variety. For the attributes of weight, durability, simplicity, and nutritional value, some level of objectivity can be used to identify the characteristics of each for every recipe. Taste and variety are obviously subjective. But the recipes in this book purposely span a wide range of tastes so that, by default, both will be covered for most any palate.

Weight is obviously straightforward, and the trail-ready measure of weight in ounces is provided for each recipe. Durability is indicated visually using a two-icon system, a single icon of a quarter-moon, identifying those recipes designed for short-duration trips (overnight in warmer weather, perhaps slightly longer if the weather is cool), and a multiphase moon icon for those appropriate for trips of any duration.

Simplicity is addressed through the challenge level assigned to each—"easy," "moderate," or "difficult"—and considers skill level required for all preparation steps, both at home and on the trail. Those recipes with a significant fraction of wholesome and nutritious ingredients are tagged with an icon of a carrot, noting them as a healthier option.

Besides the recipe attributes, serving numbers inform the trail chef as to how many people each recipe can feed so that the recipe can be scaled, if required. Perhaps less important on the trail than in camp, but nevertheless helpful to the cook, is an understanding of the time required to prepare each meal. Therefore, estimated preparation time, usually rounded to the nearest quarter-hour, is also provided. In addition, the required cooking method necessary on the trail—no-cook, pot, and frying pan—is indicated by the use of corresponding icons.

Because of their lightweight, durable nature, dehydrated ingredients are common in backpacking foods, and the recipes in this book are no different. Many dried ingredients can be purchased commercially, but it's very easy and inexpensive to do your own drying at home using a food dehydrator. Any additional effort spent in the home kitchen drying food is usually rewarded on the trail with easier preparation, improved durability, and less fuel used. Nevertheless, to further simplify their food preparation options at home, some prefer not to use home-dehydrated foods. To quickly call attention to recipes that require such ingredients, an icon depicting a dehydrator is used.

This book sorts recipes using an approach specifically designed to assist Scouts and Scouters with nearly any backpacking menu-planning scenario they are likely to encounter. While recipes are first grouped at top level by meal category, forming the main recipe chapters in the book, from there the recipes have been sub-grouped by durability, then by cooking method, which correlates closely to both challenge level and preparation time. Finally, recipes are then sub-grouped by weight per serving. Number of servings, weight data, preparation time, and challenge level are summarized in a prominent box in the sidebar of each recipe.

Supplemental Information for the Trail Cook

Material in the front and back sections of the book will assist the backpacking chef with the challenge of cooking on the trail. An important section on safety highlights common risks of trail cooking and how to help reduce the probability of an accident far from the hospital. Be safe.

Hand-in-hand with safety comes skill. An expert trail chef is far less likely to inflict injury or illness to himself or his fellow Scouts. A section on basic skills reviews the competencies that outdoor chefs should understand and master. Info on home dehydrating will help save weight and improve durability through the use of dried foods.

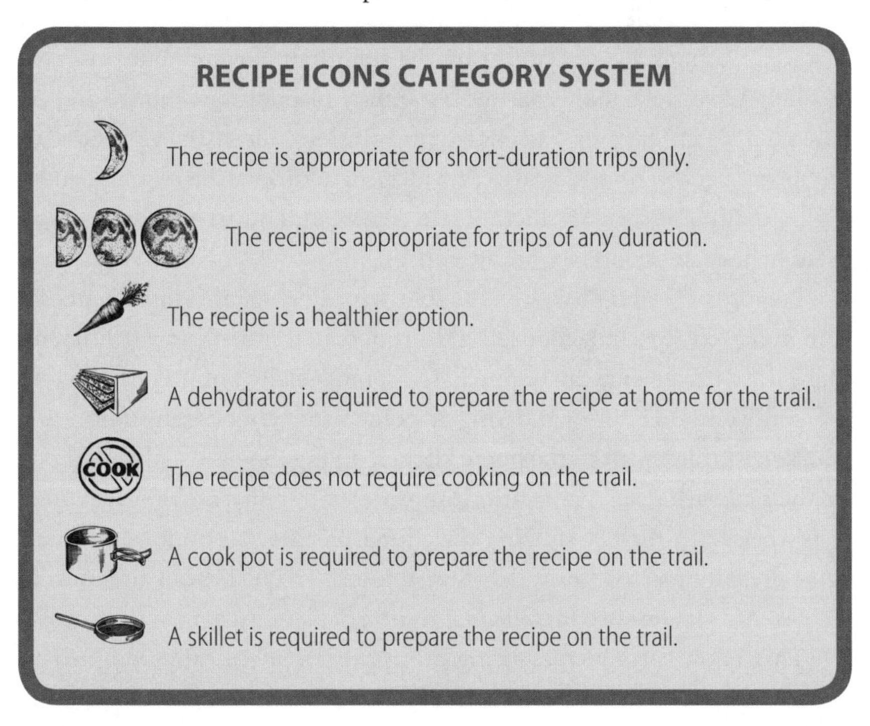

For those who have never cooked while backpacking, a detailed tutorial rounds out the front matter of the book. Based on an easy-to-prepare recipe, every step of the process is detailed, from shopping, to preparing and packing the recipe at home, to cooking the recipe on the trail, and finally, to cleaning up.

The appendices cover a wide variety of helpful information, including measurement conversions, sources of trail cooking equipment and supplies, additional resources on outdoor cooking, and techniques for reducing the environmental impact of trail cooking. Also included is a list of Boy Scout merit badge requirements related to outdoor cooking that this cookbook can help Scouts to achieve. And if you'd like to hit the nation's long-distance trails, check out the information on the National Trails System.

Healthy Pairings

Wise choices and moderation are key to maintaining a healthy diet on the trail. Moderation is usually guaranteed by the fact that there is only so much food to be found in your pack. But wise choices begin with the planning process, so when choosing recipes that lean toward higher fats and sugars, balance out your day with healthier options. This is especially critical on longer treks, when your body needs and craves high-quality fuel.

Make healthy snacks the norm, reserving fatty and sugary treats, such as that king-size candy bar, as the reward for making it up and over a grueling 12,000-foot mountain pass.

Drinks with electrolytes can be appropriate when the weather is warm and the level of exertion very high. But otherwise, make the mainstay clear, pure, cool filtered water from wild mountain streams and springs, a rare treat that few people in this day have the opportunity to experience.

Scouts take a break to filter water from a cold spring along the Appalachian Trail. *ROBERT WAGNER*

TRAIL COOKING SAFETY

Paramount to all Scouting activities is the requirement that we conduct ourselves in a safe and responsible manner at all times and in all places. It may come as a surprise to some, but cooking, whether in camp or on the trail, presents some of the more significant hazards that a Scout will face during his stay outdoors.

Most people have learned to successfully manage dangers in the home kitchen through caution and experience. But outdoor cooking presents many new and unique hazards that, if not appreciated and controlled, can cause severe injury or illness. The following information on trail cooking safety highlights the most common risks and what can be done to help reduce the probability of an accident.

While the goal should always be zero accidents, minor injuries, including cuts and burns, are common while cooking outdoors. Keep the first-aid kit handy for these. But never acceptable are more serious injuries or food-borne illness. Extreme care and caution should always be used to prevent accidents that would otherwise send your Scouts or Scouters to the hospital. This point is even more important while on trail, where the time to get to help can be measured in days.

Be careful. A razor-sharp pocket knife can go deep into your body before your brain has time to register what is happening. Fuel leaking from a pack stove can explode into a fireball, burning your face. Harmful bacteria, left alive due to improper cooking, can leave you so ill that you can't even walk.

Learn to respect every step of the cooking process. Always think about what you are about to do and ask yourself, "Is this safe?" If it isn't, or even if you are uncomfortable for reasons you don't understand, trust your instinct. Stop and determine how to do the job better, either by using more appropriate techniques and equipment or by asking others for assistance or advice. Move slowly and methodically. No matter how hungry the Scouts might be, no meal is worth compromising health and well-being.

With care and attention, any cooking risk can be managed to an acceptable level. The following list of guidelines for safety will help you do just that.

Supervision, Assistance, and Setup

- First and foremost, a responsible adult leader or mature Scout must always carefully supervise the cooking activities of less experienced Scouts, even more so when heat, sharp utensils, or raw meat are involved.
- When cooking on the trail, schedule pressure often occurs while trying to break camp in the morning, when foul weather is moving in quickly, or when nightfall is fast approaching. If you find yourself trailing, don't rush to catch up. The chances of accident and injury will only increase. And don't be a martyr, silently suffering under the burden. You'll only fatigue yourself all the more quickly. Instead, immediately enlist help from other skilled members of your troop or crew to help get the meal preparation back on track.
- Establish your cooking zone in an area well-removed from the main traffic in your trail camp. Especially at the end of a long day, with the natural desire for camaraderie and bravado, it's tempting to cook in the middle of where the action is. But pack stoves sit naturally low to the ground and are prone to being inadvertently kicked asunder in areas with a lot of activity. Move to the side of camp, and request that those who aren't assisting stay out of the cooking area.

Food Poisoning

- To decrease the probability of illness from parasites, bacteria, or viruses, all water taken from natural sources must be properly purified while on the trail. Do not assume that the heat from the cooking process will be adequate to sanitize your water. There are many high-quality and reliable devices on the market designed for water purification while backpacking. The best choice for your situation will depend on the water quality in the area you'll be visiting as well as personal preference on the method of purification.

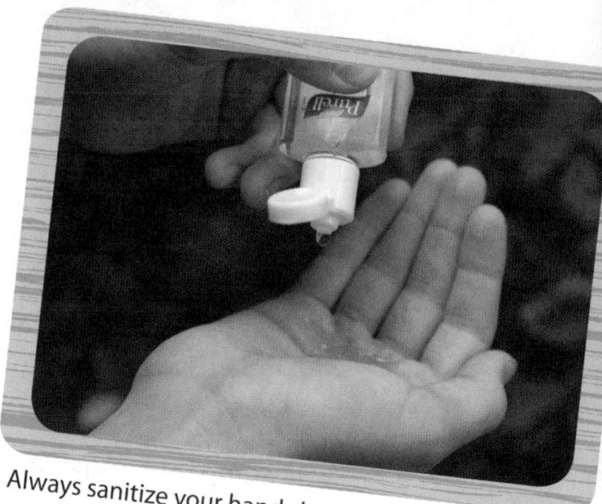

Always sanitize your hands before cooking for yourself or others, even when on the trail. CHRISTINE CONNERS

- The inside of a backpack can become toasty over the course of a long day, especially when the weather is warm. However, the surface of a backpack becomes downright hot when exposed to direct sunlight. Store foods away from the upper and rear surfaces of the backpack, deeper in the center of the pack, to reduce the temperature that the food is exposed to and to extend its shelf life.
- Do not bring raw meat or eggs on the trail unless they are to be cooked and consumed soon after leaving the trailhead. This is especially true in warm weather. Raw meats should be frozen hard, well-wrapped and thoroughly sealed, then buried deep in a well-insulated region of the backpack before heading out on the trail. Do not allow the meat to completely thaw and become warm before using. If the meat discolors, or if meat or eggs develop an off odor, do not use.
- Cold and wet weather can significantly lengthen cooking time as can high altitude, which lowers the boiling temperature of water. Consider these factors when cooking and be sure to thoroughly heat your food throughout.
- All food should be packaged tightly and securely to reduce the risk of spoilage. Loose seals on containers or ziplock bags give entry to moisture and contaminants, both of which decrease the shelf life of your food. This is especially important if packing for a long trip lasting more than a day or two. Now is not the time to cut corners: Always use high-quality ziplock bags and containers. Heavy-duty ziplock bags are recommended for foods with a rough, jagged nature that might otherwise puncture thin walls of less expensive bags.

- Certain elements of backpacking, especially when answering nature's call, require fastidious attention to the cleanliness of one's hands. Each member of the group should bring a small container of hand sanitizer, enough to last the trip, for thoroughly cleansing their hands before handling food at mealtime. This is particularly needed when water for cleaning is in short supply.
- All cookware and utensils should be carefully cleaned following each use. If greasy or smelling strongly of the meal just prepared, then keep washing. Not only will you avoid unwanted animal interest by reducing the odors, but you'll reduce the chance of any food remnants spoiling and creating a hazard next time that you cook. And don't make the common mistake of overlooking your pocket knife if you've used it to slice cheese or meats. The blade slots, grooves, and joints of a knife collect food bits that must be cleaned carefully after such use. Wipe your cookware and utensils dry following cleaning to help remove any remaining protozoa, cysts, or other nasties that may have survived the suds.
- A final line of protection: If any food smells or looks odd or if signs of mold or odd patches of discoloration are seen, discard it. Do not risk a case of food poisoning. Even the mildest case of food poisoning can be a miserable experience when you're deep in the wilderness.

Physical Dehydration

- Heavy exertion can dehydrate the body very rapidly, placing the body at increased risk of cramping, injury, and ailment. To stay properly hydrated, more than a gallon of water is easily required on hot days when trekking with a heavy backpack. When urine becomes a deeper shade of yellow, that's a sure sign you need to up the water intake. Don't rely on sense-of-thirst, which often only develops after your body has become dehydrated. Keep a water bottle or hydration pack filled and handy at all times, and get in the habit of taking frequent sips while on the trail.

- Electrolytes, such as sodium and potassium, are essential to the proper metabolic functioning of the body. When drinking large quantities of water on warm days, more electrolytes are flushed from the body through perspiration and urination and require replacement. A typical diet should provide enough sodium, but supplementation is often required to maintain adequate reserves of the other electrolytes, either through energy bars, sport drink mixes, or mineral tablets. Have these types of items available on the trail and use them, especially if you begin to feel your energy reserves quickly diminishing or you begin to cramp.

Cuts and Burns

- With many backpacking recipes, much of the cutting and chopping occurs at home and not on the trail. But an occasional recipe does require knife work at mealtime. A standard kitchen knife has no place on the trail. It is too large and dangerous for the pack. Heavy folding knives are also unnecessary. A standard pocket knife should be adequate for accomplishing any food preparation job on the trail.
- Cutting utensils are inherently dangerous, and it goes without saying that they should be handled with care. Dull blades can be more dangerous than sharper instruments. Dull knife blades can unintentionally slip much more easily when slicing or chopping, and can quickly end up in the side of your finger instead of the food you're cutting. Maintaining the sharpness of knife blades will help ensure they do what you expect them to. When slicing and chopping, always keep your hands and fingers away from the underside of the cutting edge and from in front of the blade tip.
- Backpacking stoves are small and lightweight for good reason, but that small size makes them somewhat unstable, especially when used with larger cook pots or skillets. Improve the stability by setting the stove on a solid, level surface, such as the top of a flat rock. Before leaving on the trail, check to be sure that your cookware is not too large for

use with the stove. If the stove or cookware wants to tip easily, look for a smaller pot or skillet. Use care while cooking by always bracing the pot or skillet handle with one hand while stirring with the other. If your cookware is not kept from slipping by doing this, it—and the hot food—could end up tipping onto the ground or your unprotected skin.

- Handles are easy to inadvertently snag, and so they become a frustratingly simple way of accidently tipping the pot or skillet. Use cookware that has retractable or removable handles so that they don't get in the way while the pot or skillet is on the stove.
- Stoves become red hot during use. Fortunately, they only take a few minutes to cool off because of their small size. But that small size also makes them easy to grab and move without giving it much thought. And that is where the danger lies. Inadvertently grabbing a searing hot stove from the top will leave a spectacular pattern of burns on your fingers and palm. This is sure to impress your friends, but won't be very fun while you wait for them to heal.
- Be extra cautious with plastic food bags containing hot water, as the bags can potentially tip or rupture, covering your skin in scalding liquid. Brace the bag, such as in an empty cook pot, before pouring hot water into it, then minimize handling of the bag until it cools to a safe temperature.

Fire Safety

- It is imperative that any applicable fire regulations be strictly adhered to. These are often posted at trailheads. But a surer way to gather this information is to contact the appropriate authorities for the area you are visiting. It is not uncommon for campfires to be banned while the use of backpacking stoves is permissible. In very dry conditions, any type of open fire may be banned, including stoves. Ignorance is no excuse. Make no assumptions regarding the law. The potential legal, financial, and environmental consequences are enormous to you and your group should you ignore the law or lose control of your fire.

- All cooking must be performed in a fire-safe area, clear of natural combustibles like dry leaves, grass, and trees. Instead of creating a man-made fire-safe zone about your cooking area, and potentially leaving behind the ugly evidence, take your cooking to a durable area naturally free of combustibles, such as the surface of a large, flat rock or an area of bare soil or sand. Imagine the size of the fireball that might occur should your stove leak fuel and burst into flames, then place the stove at least that far from the nearest combustibles, including overhanging trees.

This stove has been set up in a fire-safe area: the top of a huge boulder. *TED AYERS*

- Cooking fuel is an obvious hazard, both to you and to the environment. Care should always be taken when lighting your stove, no matter what type of design is used. A stove leaking fuel under pressure can produce an impressive fireball that, if you're fortunate, won't do anything more than burn the hair off your forearms. But you shouldn't let the situation get that far anyway. Before striking the match, and with the stove assembled, pressurized, and the valve closed, listen and sniff for fuel leaks. If you note a problem, repair the stove, using a maintenance kit if necessary, before proceeding. But if you are unable to repair the stove, do not use it. Better to eat a cold dinner than to burn either yourself or the forest. And always use care when starting a normally functioning stove. A stove will often flash while lighting, so keep your face well away when doing so. Understand how to properly operate your stove before attempting to use it for the first time, and especially before using it on the trail.

- Many stoves are supplied with an aluminum windscreen, and some also come with a base plate to go underneath the stove. Both are designed to help keep heat where you want it: on the pot. But both also serve an important safety function. A base plate can help prevent any remaining bits of duff from igniting under the stove while it is in use, while a windscreen can prevent windblown sparks from reaching any nearby combustibles. Use a base plate, if your stove comes with one, and always use a windscreen if the weather is gusty.

A windscreen and base plate not only conserve heat in breezy conditions but also help prevent blowing sparks and embers from escaping your fire-safe zone.
TIM CONNERS

- Keep loose and combustible items, such as jackets, sleeves, towels, plastic bags, and hair, away from the stove when it is in operation or cooling down following cooking. Alcohol stoves burn with a colorless flame that is almost impossible to see in sunlight. Without the visual cue, these stoves are notorious for burning clothing (and skin), and extra care is required for their use.

Avoid building campfires for the sole purpose of cooking while on the trail. Bring a backpacking stove for the purpose. Used properly, a stove will not leave behind evidence of its use, and, compared to a campfire, a stove poses less chance of creating a wildfire. Have filled water bottles at the ready to extinguish any flames that might otherwise threaten to escape your fire-safe zone.

Never attempt to cook in a sleeping tent. The fully enclosed walls can concentrate deadly gases and cause asphyxiation. Or the tent walls or floor could rapidly catch fire, trapping the occupants. A flat tarp, set at an angle above head-height to safely vent noxious fumes and positioned well out of range of the flames of the stove, can serve to protect the stove during rainy or snowy weather.

Allergies and Special Diets

- When planning a menu for an outing, ask your fellow Scouts and Scouters if any have food allergies or health issues that might require special dietary restrictions. Once on the trail and far from medical assistance, a severe allergic reaction could be life-threatening. At the least, a dietary reaction can make the trip very uncomfortable for the poor soul struck with such a malady. Do not assume that, because they haven't told you, none have such issues. Many recipes can be modified to meet special dietary needs while satisfying everyone else in the group. This approach can be far easier on the cook than attempting to adhere to a parallel special-requirements menu.

Wild Animals

- Animals searching for food can pose a danger to backpackers either through aggression or disease. Food bags, odorous items such as toiletries, dirty cookware and utensils left unattended, leftover food waste improperly disposed of: These all will eventually attract unwanted animal attention. Wildlife that gains access to such goodies will surely come back for more, placing these animals at risk of harm along with the people who must interact with them or remove them. A camp that is neat and clean, with food and garbage properly stored and secured, is far less attractive to the local fauna. Practice low-impact principles and adhere to any food storage regulations unique to your area, such as the requirement for bear-bagging.
- In areas with the potential for bear activity, cook and eat far downwind from your sleeping area to reduce the chance of it becoming of nocturnal interest to bruins looking to satisfy their incessant hunger. Better yet, pause for an early dinner while still on the trail, then walk the final mile or two to your stopping point for the day. By doing so, you'll leave the enticing aromas well behind.

No list can cover every danger lurking in every situation, and the above is surely no exception. But by learning to cook with a mind fixated on safety, few circumstances will catch you ill-prepared or by surprise.

BASIC SKILLS AND EQUIPMENT FOR THE TRAIL CHEF

Cooking a great meal out of a backpack might seem magical, perhaps impossible. It's neither, of course. And a strong foundation in the fundamentals of outdoor cooking in general, and trail cooking in particular, will make it all the more likely you'll be successful. With this in mind, the following section covers the essential skills for cooking when one's kitchen is in one's backpack.

Planning for the Obvious . . . and the Unexpected

- If you are new to trail cooking, keep your backpacking menu simple, especially for longer trips. Raise the challenge level only after you've become more skilled and confident in your abilities. Taking on more than a person can manage is a common mistake, and the botched meal that results is sure to disappoint not only the one doing the work but also the famished stomachs depending on the chef.
- Foul weather adds a powerful variable to the outdoor cooking equation. And bugs and wild animals further distract by keeping you on the defensive. Prior to any outing, weather and critters should be considered and planned for appropriately. Be realistic about what

Here are some of the foods gathered for a weeklong trek in the High Sierra. TIM CONNERS you can handle under the circumstances likely to be encountered. The more trying the conditions, the simpler the menu should be.

- Enlist help and divide cooking and cleanup duties among Scouts and leaders to lighten the load. Discuss roles and responsibilities in advance so there is no confusion or push-back when it comes time to engage. The recipes in this book use numerical sequencing for the instructions. Use these to best assign tasks to the helpers.
- They are often enthusiastic to help, but younger Scouts can require much more supervision. Make sure you can manage the additional workload when assigning tasks to the tenderfoots. If cooking in inclement weather or under an extreme time crunch, there will come a better time to engage the assistance of the inexperienced chefs.
- The younger the Scouts, the more they tend to openly grumble about their food, even when it is obviously awesome to everyone else. And after a long day on the trail, complaining is the last thing you want to hear. A powerful way to avoid this is to include your Scouts, especially the younger ones, in the meal-planning process. By giving them a voice, they become stakeholders in the meal's success and are more likely to enjoy, not just tolerate, the results.
- Groceries account for a large fraction of cost on most outings, and parents appreciate when efforts are made to keep expenses reasonable. However, cost cutting can be taken to an extreme, with ingredients of such low quality that it's painfully obvious, meal after meal. Be frugal with other people's money, but be prudent about cost-cutting measures. Spend the extra money when it makes sense. It's justifiable, and the Scouts and Scouters will appreciate the difference.
- Any dish can end its short life tragically dumped in the dirt by fate or accident. Many miles from the nearest road, Plan B's are hard to come by in the wilderness. If mealtime goes awry, you'll have no choice but to re-plan the menu for the remainder of the trip to offset the lost food. One such event shouldn't cause undue hardship to you and your crew.

Mosquitoes are found everywhere in the summertime. Head nets maintain the sanity of these cooks as they prepare dinner in the Colorado Rockies. MARY HIBBARD

- Now if a bear happens to abscond with the entire food stash, or the meal bag is inadvertently dropped over a cliff into a raging river, that's another story. Quickly take stock of the group's remaining inventory, including energy bars and any personal stashes. Now is not the time to horde. If reserves are low in this scenario, carefully plan how to distribute the remaining food and be prepared to head straight back to civilization, recognizing that a couple of days without grub never hurt anyone. As your stomach grumbles, don't forget to stay properly hydrated. Your body needs the water more than the food, and it can help lessen the hunger pains until that wondrous moment when you finally make it off the trail and into the nearest pizza parlor.

Menu Selection and Preparation at Home

- The typical adult or older teen will eat no more than about 1½ pounds of packed food per day, assuming that most, if not all, of the food has been dried. This weight value easily doubles or even triples when carrying fresh foods or canned goods. For a long trek spanning a week, about 10 pounds of dried food will be adequate for most older teens or adults, less than this for the younger Scouts. In contrast, if canned goods comprised most of the food items, the weight would increase to nearly 30 pounds per person, an unacceptably heavy amount. Total pack weight should not exceed one-quarter of body weight to avoid over-stressing joints and muscles, and food should not exceed one-third of pack weight to leave adequate room for other critical gear. For a 40-pound pack, then, foods other than dried generally become too heavy once the trip length exceeds a few days.

- One-pot meals are the backbone of most trail menus because less equipment, fuel, and effort are required for preparation compared to multicourse meals. But don't think that a one-pot recipe makes the meal boring. There are many outstanding one-pot recipes, including those in this book, that stand perfectly well on their own.
- It's easier to prepare for a backpacking trip by multiplying good recipes for use on more than one day instead of preparing a unique recipe for every meal. But even a great recipe can become tiring if eaten too often, so balance convenience with variety when planning your menu.
- Most backpacking recipes are easy to prepare on the trail, but many require accurate final preparation directions regarding the amount of water necessary to rehydrate or the addition of final ingredients, such as oils. Because of this, it is important that the on-trail directions be included with the recipe. Don't forget them. When using a recipe with final on-trail preparation steps, transcribe the information on a small slip of paper and include it with the food as you pack.
- For overnight trips, special food preparation is usually unnecessary. With plenty of room in the backpack, canned goods, fresh fruits and vegetables, and larger and heavier cooking gear can be managed. If you do bring canned goods on short trips, don't forget the can opener. Many are the stories of frustrated individuals who've had to resort to opening their cans with blows from rocks.
- For longer trips spanning more than a few days, it becomes difficult to justify the substantial weight penalty associated with foods that have not been dried. A larger portion of your meals should consist of dried foods on treks like these. For trips spanning four days or more, almost all foods should be dried, for reasons of weight and durability.

- Water accounts for most of the weight of fresh fruits and vegetables, about 80 percent of which can be eliminated through drying. For canned goods, the fraction saved is even higher. The can itself accounts for as much as one-quarter of the weight of canned goods. By eliminating the can, draining the liquid, drying the contents in a dehydrator, and repackaging the food in plastic food bags for the trail, as much as 90 percent of the initial weight can be saved.
- When bringing along dried foods originally prepackaged in boxes, such as rice mixes, repackage the contents in ziplock bags for the trail. By removing the packaging, trash is reduced and some weight is saved in the process. More importantly, ziplock bags pack more efficiently than boxes because the bags are free to mold to the confines of the inside of the pack. Be sure to clip any relevant directions from the box and place them along with the food in the ziplock bag.
- Package dry foods and ingredients in high-quality ziplock bags, just large enough to do the job. The more aromatic or jagged the food, the thicker the bag's plastic walls should be. Heavy-duty freezer-type ziplock bags are appropriate for most jobs. Ingredients packaged individually for a given recipe can be gathered together into a larger-size ziplock to create a self-contained meal. Less expensive or generic-brand bags tend to have thinner walls and less robust seals, so use these with caution.
- Label ziplock bags with the recipe name and the date packaged using a permanent marker. Other useful information to note includes the number of servings, the day to use the food on the trail, and any simple instructions, like the amount of water required. Squeeze out as much air as possible, then seal tightly. Recheck the seal to be sure it is securely shut, then store the bags in the refrigerator or freezer until ready to pack before heading to the trail.
- If a bear-proof food canister is not required for the area you'll be visiting, gather all meals together into a large, sturdy food sack for the backpack. Avoid placing your food at the bottom of the pack, where

it can be subjected to unnecessary weight from heavy items above it. Instead, position the bag in the center of the pack, close to the forward (strap-side) wall of the backpack. This positions the food in a less compressed and cooler area of the pack while keeping the center of gravity farther forward, a more comfortable location for the backpacker.

- Lightweight and durable, condiment packets are an excellent way to liven up foods on the trail. Ketchup, taco sauce, soy sauce, barbecue sauce, hot sauce, relish, mayonnaise, mustard, honey, syrups, jellies, lemon juice, grated Parmesan cheese, and dried red pepper are some of the choices available. Save any extras from restaurants that you frequent or purchase online in bulk from wholesale suppliers.
- Fresh butter is suitable for short treks but lacks durability for longer trips. Dried butter substitutes, such as Butter Buds, are an easy, good-tasting, and durable alternative for many recipes.
- Use an accurate kitchen scale when preparing for the trail. Measure each of the packaged food items to be sure the final weight is close to that specified by the recipe. (If it isn't close, this would be a telltale sign that something is amiss, either with the recipe or the preparation. Troubleshoot the problem before you hit the trail.) A bath scale is valuable for determining the combined weight of the packed gear, to help in keeping the total weight of the pack below target, and for equally distributing the gear and food load between the Scouts.

A kitchen scale is invaluable for accurately dividing large recipes into individual servings.
CHRISTINE CONNERS

- When packing equipment for the trail, use a checklist. By doing so, you are less likely to forget a critical piece of gear. Review the list after each trip and modify it as required as you gain experience. Checklists tend to be very personal, and you'll soon discover that no two ever seem to be the same.
- To decrease the risk of their failure in a situation when you can least afford it, test recipes at home or on short trips before relying on them during longer or more challenging expeditions.
- Don't neglect nutrition on the trail. It's important to balance fats, carbohydrates, and proteins while backpacking. Carbohydrates provide a more rapidly available source of energy than do fats, and by combining the two, short- and long-term energy levels are more likely to be sustained. Proteins are valuable for extending the utilization of carbohydrates. Fats at suppertime are particularly useful in cold weather as they help the body sleep more warmly throughout the night. Constipation is a common problem on the trail, but a fiber-rich diet, along with plenty of water, will help maintain regularity. Choose healthier fats, such as olive oil, when cooking, and avoid filling up on empty calories from simple sugars.

Preparation on the Trail

- Review and understand your recipe before commencing preparation in the field. You are less likely to make a critical mistake if you do so. And be sure you have everything needed before starting to cook by first gathering all ingredients and cooking utensils together.
- Purified water is an obvious requirement during the high exertion of walking the trail. But a surprisingly large amount is also required in camp for cooking, cleaning, and replenishing the body's reserves. To minimize wilderness impact, a trail camp should never be established next to a water source unless a dedicated area has been created for the purpose. Of course, one drawback to camping away from water

is the need to haul it from the source back to camp. For this reason, a collapsible plastic water carrier or dromedary bag, with a capacity of a gallon or more, is an ideal way of keeping a supply of water close at hand. The carrier can be quickly filled with raw water at the source then purified as needed at camp.

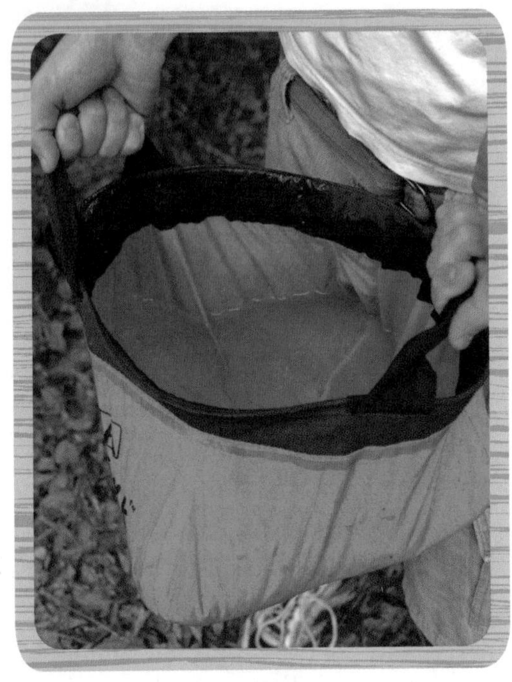

A lightweight, collapsible carrier is a convenient way to keep a large quantity of water at the ready in your trail camp. *CHRISTINE CONNERS*

- An extension of the previous point is to avoid the vicinity of water altogether when stopping for the night, and instead, look for those out-of-the-way areas with incredible vistas . . . and fewer bugs. Often called "dry camping," the idea is to purposely overload on water, with reserves adequate for the night and following morning, then continue on the trail to a campsite with a grand view or other redeeming quality. This is a liberating technique that moves campsite wear-and-tear away from the more heavily used water sources, while opening up a vastly larger world of camping opportunities along the trail.
- Dried milk powders are notorious for clumping during reconstitution, more so when the water is cold. Of course, warm water, and therefore warm milk, does not make for a good bowl of cold cereal in the morning. One method for avoiding clumping is to first add a small amount of water to the powder in a drinking cup, stirring

until it becomes a thick, smooth paste. The remainder of the water, even if cold, can then be added with no resulting clumping. Part- or whole-fat milk powders generally taste and reconstitute better than nonfat varieties. Whole milk powder, such as Nestle's Nido, can often be found in the Hispanic food section at the grocery store.

- Carry a selection of favorite spices on the trail to satisfy individual preferences. Small containers are available from backpacking suppliers specifically for this purpose.
- Etch water bottles, containers, or mugs in measures of a cup and fractions of a cup for determining required amounts of water when cooking on the trail. Many transparent or translucent water containers come premarked with measuring lines specifically for this purpose. Learn to estimate one teaspoon and one tablespoon as measured using your backpacking spoon.
- Though likely to be necessary when carrying fresh vegetables and fruits, chopping and slicing isn't required for most trail recipes. When knife work is called for, the clean bottom of the cook pot or lid makes an adequate substitute for a cutting board.
- With the modern cooking gear and methods now available, it can be hard to imagine how much effort went into camp cooking in the not-too-distant past. Cooking pits and trenches, roaring fires, wooden tripods and cooking boards all had a reason and a place at one time but left behind a scar in the wilderness that was slow to heal. With modern gear, these methods and techniques are no longer necessary on the trail. Use tools and equipment to minimize your impact to the trail environment and to truly leave no trace.

Managing the Heat

- Become familiar with your cooking stove and how much fuel is required to prepare a meal. Don't forget fuel required for heating water for coffee, tea, and other hot drinks. Bring extra for contingency, especially if the weather is to be wet or cold. Monitor fuel use while on the trail. Test your cooking equipment before leaving on your trip, looking for clogging or leaks. Be sure your gear is in good working order, and carry a repair kit for contingency. Maintenance kits are very lightweight and take little room in the pack.

- Use a windscreen and, if your stove comes with one, a base plate to improve fuel efficiency. Both reflect heat back onto the pot or skillet and should be employed even if the weather isn't windy. Likewise, place the lid on your pot when cooking to help retain heat.
- Pack ovens are wonderful devices that open up a variety of baked food options on the trail. But if your pack oven uses water to control the heat, never allow the oven to boil dry. If it does, the plastic oven bag is likely to melt and create a true mess in your cook pot.
- Some plastics used in food storage bags may begin to soften at temperatures close to the boiling point of water. There is growing debate over the safety implications of such. However, rehydrating foods in storage bags using hot water, as opposed to boiling the bag, is generally considered safe because the temperature of boiled water very quickly falls off once the water is removed from the heat source and introduced to the bag. If rehydrating foods in storage bags using hot water is a concern to you, simply use a cook pot instead. It's a messier approach, but it's an easy alternative.
- An option to rehydrating foods in plastic storage bags is to use roasting bags instead. These are specifically designed for safe use at temperatures much higher than the boiling point of water and are correspondingly more expensive. While these bags can't be sealed in ziplock fashion, the open necks can be twisted and tied, with the top of the bag positioned so as not to collect steam or water.
- The boiling point of water decreases with altitude, dropping by nearly 20°F, for example, at 12,000 feet elevation compared to sea

level. With the decrease in water temperature, foods will take longer to cook, requiring more time on the stove and more fuel. Bring extra fuel for contingency at high altitude and be prepared to stir often and to sample your food more frequently to be sure it's ready to serve.

Dealing with the Weather

- Perhaps the most challenging of all outdoor cooking situations involves rain. In a heavy downpour, the only options may be to cease and desist and wait it out, serve no-cook foods, or move the stove under a fire-safe tarp, if you're fortunate to have one. Never cook in a sleeping tent.
- In light rain, the pot itself, along with a windscreen, is usually adequate for shielding the burner, allowing cooking to commence and continue. This is also a moment when you'll be glad to have that box of waterproof matches.

A light rain won't stop dinner when using a gasoline-fueled pack stove. *TED AYERS*

A brutal layer of rime ice makes a nice backdrop for this propane stove that's been stabilized by shoving its base into the snow. CURT WHITE

- Snow presents its own unique challenges to cooking; the most difficult is usually locating a decent place to set the stove. In mountainous areas, the tops of large rocks or boulders can often be found free of snow as can the ground along the downwind side of the same. In areas with rapidly changing topography, it usually is just a matter of time before a snow-free area can be found along the trail. If snow stretches as far as the eye can see, but isn't deep, a suitable spot can be cleared by hand and foot. Place the stove on a pot lid set into packed snow if it's deep.

Keeping It Clean While Cooking on the Trail

- Maintain a close eye on your food while cooking so that it doesn't burn. Charred food is difficult to remove and requires much more time, water, and detergent during cleanup.
- Use dishwashing liquid sparingly during cleanup, just enough to do the job. Only detergents that are biodegradable should be used outdoors. Bring a small piece of scrub pad for tackling stuck-on foods. Clean, coarse sand or small scree can also be used along with a little water for cleaning the insides of your pots and pans, provided they aren't coated in nonstick material.
- Grease and stuck-on food is cut more easily, and with less detergent, when using warm water. If you can spare the fuel, throw a little water

in the soiled pot or skillet, warm the water briefly, splash it around, then let the cookware sit for a few minutes before scrubbing.

- Dispose of wash and rinse water, also called "gray water," in a manner acceptable to your particular area. Never dump gray water directly into a stream or lake. If the rinse water contains large bits of food, strain these out and dispose of them with your pack trash. If the area you are visiting is particularly sensitive ecologically or contains wild animals that may be especially interested in your food, then gray water should be disposed of just like fecal matter—in a cat hole covered with several inches of soil and located at least 200 feet from the nearest water source. Always follow any special local regulations regarding waste disposal.
- Dirty cookware left to lie will eventually attract bugs and wild animals. To avoid such interest, ensure that all utensils have been washed and rinsed before leaving base camp during the day or when retiring for the evening.
- Minimize the use of aluminum foil, which tends to shred into small pieces that are easy to miss during cleanup and which remain unsightly for years. Likewise, keep a close eye on smaller trash items, such as empty condiment packs, bouillon cube wrappers, and the like. A good practice is to immediately place small trash items in a larger bag before they are dropped and forgotten.
- Reclaimed ziplock bags, used to carry food for your trip but now empty following the meal, make excellent trash receptacles. Squeezed to remove air then sealed tightly, they can be placed bag-in-bag to isolate aromatic and rotting waste. If carrying your dried food in ziplocks, you are unlikely to find yourself short on excellent trash containers.
- Bear-proof food canisters are the best option when visiting areas with high bruin activity. They are neither inexpensive nor lightweight, but the peace of mind and convenience they bring over conventional bear-

bagging can't be overstated. In fact, in some areas and parks, their use is required by law.

This bear canister weighs less than 3 pounds yet holds up to a week's worth of food for one backpacker. It is impervious to bear assault. *CHRISTINE CONNERS*

- If bear-bagging is the only option, use a large sack to pack all foods along with any aromatics that could attract animal attention, including trash, toothpaste, deodorant, and sunscreen. All items should be in waterproof storage bags, such as ziplocks, to keep them dry in case of rain. Be sure to use a stout sack to hold your stash, beefy enough to suspend it all off the ground without rupturing like a piñata in the middle of the night. Also required is a long, strong hanging rope, at least 40 feet in length, to hoist it all. As any experienced backpacker knows, the perfect bear-bagging tree is a cruel myth. But try to find it anyway, one with a thick tree limb 15 or more feet from, and parallel to, the ground. Toss the rope over the limb and hoist the food bag. The bag should hang at least 6 feet off the trunk of the tree so that a climbing bear can't reach it. Likewise, the bag should rest several feet under the branch from which it hangs. Securely tie off the loose end of the rope to a neighboring tree.

Proper bear-bagging can take a lot of effort but is an effective way to thwart all but the most persistent Yogi. *WAYNE KODAMA*

- In some areas, the bears are smart enough to defeat the bagging techniques described above, and the more-involved process of counterbalancing may be required. Even that may not stop Yogi. However, if the bears in the area are this intelligent, local regulations most likely require the use of a bear-proof canister anyway.

Key Equipment for Trail and Home

- All backpackers seem to have a strong personal preference regarding stoves, and there are persuasive pros and cons for each design. There are four major classes of the most common trail stoves: gasoline, alcohol, propane canister, and solid fuel. Gasoline stoves, some of which also burn kerosene, diesel, or even jet fuel, operate under pressure, generate tremendous heat, and work well at all altitudes. Gasoline stoves are arguably the best option for frying, especially when using larger pans. Alcohol stoves operate unpressurized and are very compact and lightweight. They are most useful for preparing single servings in a small metal cup or pot, and are not well-suited for cooking for larger groups. Propane stoves are also very lightweight and compact, with excellent simmering capability and heat output. But they are less stable then most gasoline stoves, and the fuel canisters are bulky. The fuel remaining in the canister can also be difficult to judge, making it more challenging to manage fuel reserves. Solid fuel stoves use combustible tablets and are perhaps the lightest and simplest to use. But, like alcohol stoves, they work best for heating water in small quantities and not for cooking over an extended period of time. Fuel tablets may have a strong, somewhat off odor requiring layers of packaging to prevent transfer to other gear.
- Your cookware must be well matched to your stove and to the types of recipes you'd like to prepare. If all members of your group pack their own lightweight alcohol stoves, for instance, then a single-serving metal cup for each is all that would be required for cookware. However, for larger groups, and recipes that make more than one serving, a true pot and sturdy stove will be necessary. And if frying is on the

The four primary types of pack stoves, from left to right: alcohol, propane, gasoline, and solid fuel.
TIM CONNERS

menu, you'll also need a lid that can serve as a skillet.

- The selection of backpacking cookware is large and somewhat bewildering. But assuming that you plan to cook more than single servings, in quantity for the troop or crew, and would like to occasionally do some frying, all you'll need is a simple pot and multifunction lid. For packability and safety, select gear that has retractable or removable handles. Pots of about 2½-quart capacity are very good for handling most six-serving recipes or less. Larger pots rapidly become too massive and unstable for most stoves, unnecessarily large for most backpack recipes, and more difficult to pack.
- Cookware comes in an assortment of metals and coatings, and some are sold as sets specifically designed to work with certain stoves. Aluminum is the least expensive material, but also the least durable. Anodized aluminum is a tougher variant but slightly more expensive. Stainless steel is rugged but tends to be heavier. Titanium alloys are extremely light and tough but are also significantly more expensive than the other options. Nonstick surfaces definitely make cleanup easier in the wilderness, but some coatings are prone to damage and can eventually begin to flake off. The final choice regarding materials and coatings comes down to personal preference and budget.
- A pack oven isn't required, but it can definitely broaden one's repertoire by opening up a world of baking options on the trail. A lightweight and inexpensive insert, the pack oven is an ingenious modification

of the simple trivet, turning a cook pot into a double-boiler oven in water-based units, like the BakePacker. Breads, pancakes, and desserts are baked in high-temperature plastic roasting bags. The results are wonderful, and cleanup is easy. Several of the recipes in this book call for a pack oven. If you haven't used one before, consider trying it. Pack ovens can require a significant amount of time for baking, but if you have the fuel to spare, they are simple to use and a lot of fun.

- Don't forget cooking and serving utensils for the trail. A short, wooden spoon is ideal for stirring. A small plastic spatula is a must for frying pancakes and other foods that require flipping. And a collapsible ladle makes serving your group much less messy. Pack all your cook gear into a mesh bag of appropriate size to allow the equipment to breathe and dry when it is in the backpack.

An array of backpacking cooking containers, from left to right: titanium, stainless steel, nonstick coated aluminum, and anodized aluminum. CHRISTINE CONNERS

- At home, a blender is essential for pureeing chunky foods if they are to produce smooth fruit and sauce leathers. A food processor is handy for slicing or chopping foods to a uniform consistency prior to drying. And a food scale is invaluable for weighing ingredients and evenly subdividing a recipe into smaller serving sets.
- A food dehydrator is indispensible for vastly expanding the range of trail cooking options, for adapting your favorite home recipes for the trail, and for maximizing and customizing the nutrition content of your trail foods. It is a surprisingly easy appliance to use. For more information, see the next section, where dried foods and dehydration are given exclusive treatment.

REDUCING WEIGHT AND IMPROVING DURABILITY WITH DRIED FOODS

Whether performed at a factory for common items found at the grocery store, or done at home for use on the trail, the reason for drying foods is the same: Water makes up most of the weight of many food items and is an essential prerequisite for spoilage. So by removing the water through the process of drying, the food becomes much lighter and longer lasting. Dried foods are also more resistant to rough handling compared to those with a high water content. For all of these reasons, the process of drying food provides benefits that are ideal for backpackers.

Freeze-drying and dehydrating are the two primary techniques used to dry foods for the trail. Reconstitution is the process of rehydrating dried food back to its original state. On the trail, this is usually done using hot water, although cold water often works, given enough time.

Freeze-drying is performed commercially using expensive equipment to remove moisture through a rapid deep-freezing process. Most of the prepackaged meal options available at outdoor shops have been freeze-dried. Just like entrees found in the grocer's freezer, freeze-dried meals are a convenient option for the backpacker who is short on time or who prefers to minimize the cooking effort. However, freeze-dried meals have some disadvantages: They are expensive per serving, the packages are often bulky for the quantity of food provided, and the serving sizes can be awkward for the actual group size. While many freeze-dried meals are quite tasty, some aren't; costly surprises can await the backpacker on the trail unless each menu selection has been sampled previously. All of these disadvantages can make freeze-dried meals less desirable, especially when packing for the trail with a large group of Scouts.

Dehydrating is the process of using low heat over a period of hours or days to slowly and gently remove moisture from food. It is a simple and inexpensive process, and it can be performed readily at home using an appliance called a food dehydrator. A high-quality home food dehydrator can be purchased new for about the same cost as a good blender. Dehydrators come in two primary designs: one using stackable round trays with a blower at either the top or bottom of the unit, the other using a rectangular cabinet and slide-out trays over which warm air is blown. Each design has its strong points, depending on the task, but either type will perform well when drying foods for the trail. All models provide some method of adjusting the temperature, and fine-mesh screens are usually included to permit drying of small food items, such as rice, that would otherwise fall through the trays. Additional accessories can make the drying process more convenient but aren't required for the recipes in this book.

Dehydrating foods and ingredients at home allows an endless variety of your favorite recipes to be customized for the trail. Serving sizes and amounts can be tailored to the preferences of your troop or crew. And to top it off, the ingredients shrink dramatically in size once dry, taking up less volume once packed. For all of these reasons, combined with the cost-effective nature of home drying, dehydrated foods are often a great option when preparing a menu for Scout backpacking trips.

Home-dehydrated peas on the left and commercially freeze-dried peas on the right. CHRISTINE CONNERS

Entire books have been written about the art of food dehydrating, but that doesn't mean you must read one before being successful. The finer points of drying food are certainly worth learning, but they often relate to preparing food for storage times longer than what would be needed for a typical backpacking trip or to foods that are less common on the trail. You should understand the nuances of your own dehydrator, of course, to help assure safe use and predictable results. But by becoming familiar with the following list of tips and recommendations specific to drying foods at home for use on the trail, you'll be ready to tackle most any backpacking menu.

Steps for Maximizing Shelf Life and Improving Food Quality

- Thoroughly clean and dry your hands, preparation surfaces, cooking utensils, and dehydrating trays before commencing to minimize the chance of contaminating your food.
- Properly dried and sealed meats have a shelf life measured in weeks, whereas fruits, vegetables, and grains can last a year or more. Remember: The more moisture or oils remaining in the food being dried, the shorter its shelf life will be. Refrigeration greatly extends the life of foods once they've been dried, freezing even more so. Sealing tightly in high-quality food storage bags is necessary to maximize the longevity and taste of dried foods.
- In very humid kitchen environments, dry the foods as usual, place in airtight containers for a few days to give any remaining moisture time to redistribute, then return the food to the drying trays for another round. This is an effective way of reducing the probability of spoilage due to mold.
- Prior to drying cooked ground beef, begin by using lean meat then allow the fried beef to drain in a colander. Finally, rinse the meat in hot water or pat it with a paper towel. Removing as much fat and oils as possible helps to extend the shelf life of any meat.

- Always closely inspect your dried foods before packing for your trip and before cooking once on the trail. Any patches of discoloration or molding, or an odd aroma, is an indication that the food has begun to spoil and should be discarded.

Planning for Drying

- Many food items can be dried overnight, but as much as a full day or more may be needed to dehydrate some foods, especially thick purees or leathers. If a lot of drying will be required for an upcoming trip, consider the capacity of your dehydrator and be sure to set aside enough time to do the entire job. It can take more than a week to dry food for a troop heading out on a long excursion.
- Dried foods tend to pack a lot of nutrients per ounce, and this is especially true of fruit leathers. Some fruits make better-tasting leathers than others, and some combinations are truly wonderful. Try apple-and-berry combos, for instance. Some fruits, like blueberries, produce a better texture when blended with other fruits before drying.
- The kitchen oven is naturally attractive for drying because of its large capacity, provided that the door can be held open slightly to allow moisture to escape. But the lowest achievable temperature on many ovens is much higher than that recommended for drying nonmeat items. Some ovens do reach down to the range recommended for drying meats, but the unit may not be able to accurately hold the temperatures there. Before using your oven to dry large batches of meats, first understand its capabilities in the required temperature range.
- Foods containing high-fructose corn syrups, such as some canned fruits or pie fillings, can be impossible to dry, forever remaining very sticky to the touch. If attempting to dehydrate these types of foods, the results are likely to be disappointing. Read the ingredient label and avoid drying such foods.

Preparing Foods for Drying

- The more finely chopped the ingredients and the more consistent the sizes of the pieces, the more uniformly they will dehydrate and the better they will reconstitute at camp. Also ensure that pieces are spaced evenly on the drying trays for better air circulation.
- Don't mix different types of highly aromatic foods in the same drying batch to avoid intermingling flavors. Same holds true when mixing odorous foods with less aromatic types. As an example, it would be unadvisable to dry garlic and onions with a batch of fruit leathers.
- When drying sauce for spaghetti or soup on the trail, use a blender to puree chunky blends into a smooth consistency before drying. Texture can be introduced back to the sauces and soups at camp by adding dried vegetables and the like at the time of cooking.
- Thick liquids, such as spaghetti sauces and purees, can be dried in shallow pools on parchment paper, cut to the proper shape for your trays, or on reusable liners specifically designed for this purpose. Depending on the design of your dehydrator, very runny liquids are sometimes best dried in solid plastic trays specially made for your unit.
- Darkening of fruit and vegetables during and following drying naturally occurs due to oxidation. This doesn't affect the taste of the food, but can be surprising to the uninitiated. There are several ways to reduce or eliminate

A fully loaded dehydrator ready for action. From top to bottom: parboiled couscous, brown rice, quinoa pasta, spelt pasta, black beans, kidney beans, and pinto beans. *TIM CONNERS*

the occurrence of oxidation when drying, but a reasonably effective and easy method is to soak sliced fruits and vegetables for five minutes in a bath of ¼ cup lemon juice to 1 quart water prior to drying.

- Blanching is the process of lightly steaming or boiling, but not thoroughly cooking, fruits or vegetables prior to dehydrating. Blanching is beneficial in that it can extend a food's shelf life and improve its appearance once dried. It can also help to speed the rehydration process for some foods. But it is not required, especially if the trip you're preparing for will occur within the next couple of months. Blanching produces no benefit to onions, tomatoes, and mushrooms, which have naturally long shelf lives and stable appearance when dried.
- Precooking, also known as parboiling, pasta and rice then drying in the dehydrator will greatly reduce cooking and reconstitution time on the trail. When parboiling, it even becomes possible to have excellent cold pasta and rice salads on the trail because many parboiled foods can fully reconstitute even with cold water.
- Corn, legumes (peas and beans for example), and root crops (carrots, in particular) should always be thoroughly cooked before drying for the trail. They will not dry or reconstitute satisfactorily otherwise.
- Jerkies generally begin with raw meat and are preserved both through the drying and heavy salting process. Regular unsalted meats can also be dried, but should be thoroughly cooked before doing so. Slice or chop thinly after cooking, rinse under hot water to remove oils, then pat dry before dehydrating.

Maintaining the Proper Drying Environment

- Typical drying temperatures range from the upper 90s to low 100s°F for drying fragile leafy vegetables, through 125°F for most chopped or sliced vegetables, to 135°F for fruits and purees, to 155°F and higher for meat jerkies. Follow the specific guidelines and settings that come with your dehydrator.

Most vegetables, including the salsa shown here, dry best at a moderate temperature, about 125°F.
CHRISTINE CONNERS

- It may be tempting to crank the temperature beyond recommended to hasten the drying process, but there's a good reason for keeping to the specified range. When setting the temperature too high with fruits and vegetables, not only are healthful enzymes potentially destroyed, but the outer surface of the food pieces can rapidly dry and harden, trapping moisture in the interior and leading to rapid spoilage. By drying at lower temperatures, the dehydration process progresses more uniformly from outside to in. But don't take the temperature below the recommended range: The dehydration process can take so long that your food items would actually begin to spoil before drying is completed.
- When drying foods that tend to clump, such as rice, break up the clusters after a half-day or so of dehydrating, then redistribute. This will hasten the remaining process and help ensure more uniform drying. If your dehydrator is new to you, check the progress of the drying every few hours to learn the subtleties. Rotate or restack trays to keep the drying uniform.
- Some foods retain a leathery and pliable texture once fully dried, whereas other types of foods become very crisp. With a little experience, you'll find that you rarely under-dry food. The instruction manual that comes with your dehydrator can help you identify the drying characteristics of a large variety of foods to help you get it right the first time.

Packaging Dried Foods

- Quality ziplock bags with a sturdy seal are excellent for storing dehydrated foods. Pack a few extra bags for the trail just in case a seal breaks or a seam ruptures on a bag holding your dried foods.

These rings of spaghetti sauce were dried in a round dehydrator and then pulverized in a food processor before packaging in heavy-duty ziplock bags for the trail. CHRISTINE CONNERS

- Remove fruit leather while it is still warm and pliable but not sticky. If overdried or allowed to cool, the leather may become brittle and more difficult to roll, though certainly still edible. Roll fruit leathers individually on sheets of wax paper to prevent sticking.
- Vacuum sealing is not recommended for storage because the jagged edges of dried foods can puncture the tightly compressed walls of the vacuum bag, defeating the original objective of an airtight seal, and permitting the entry of moisture from the air.

Bringing Your Dried Food Back to Life on the Trail

- Some dehydrated foods can be slower to rehydrate than others while cooking. And dehydrated foods tend to rehydrate more slowly than their freeze-dried counterparts. Don't expect all dehydrated foods to return to the same predried state once rehydrated. Many do not, being slightly smaller or chewier. But this is inconsequential to most recipes since the goal is soft and tasty, not pretty.

- The best method for reconstituting your dried food depends on the specific item and how it was dried. An extended simmer or boil is usually required for foods that were not thoroughly cooked prior to drying, such as fresh vegetables. Foods that were precooked prior to drying are usually restored by simply pouring hot water over the dried food in a cup, then setting it aside for an appropriate amount of time, covering the cup to help trap heat. Some precooked foods restore well using cold water, although the time for reconstitution takes longer than when using hot water. The recipes in this book specify the method most appropriate for the foods being rehydrated.

Dried sauces will fully rehydrate on the trail even when using cold water, as here. *CHRISTINE CONNERS*

Rehydration occurs more rapidly when using hot water, as in the case for this meal in a cook pot just removed from the stove. *DAVID LATTNER*

Not all trail recipes require dehydrating foods at home, but many require dried foods of some sort, whether purchased at the grocery store or online. There are several web-based retailers of dried ingredients, and the types of foods now available are truly incredible. Check out the list of suppliers in Appendix B and challenge your creativity.

STEP-BY-STEP TRAIL COOKING TUTORIAL

This section takes the new trail chef through a great backpacking recipe suitable for two or three Scouts or Scouters. Rayado Rice and Chicken comes from Troop 809 of the Greater Saint Louis Area Council, created while preparing for a trek to Philmont Scout Ranch. The total packed weight is about 15 ounces.

Follow this tutorial from start to finish. The recipe is easy and enjoyable and takes only about 15 minutes to prepare. With it, you can also learn firsthand how to prepare dried ingredients for the trail and why they are so valuable for backpacking. Afterward, you'll be ready to take on any of the other terrific trail recipes that await in the following pages.

Rayado Rice and Chicken

First, gather the ingredients you'll need:

1 (6-ounce) box Uncle Ben's Country Inn Chicken Rice mix

1 (7-ounce) pouch Tyson Premium Chunk White Chicken Breast

6 ounces (about 1⅓ cups) fresh or frozen green peas, if dehydrating yourself, or . . .

If not dehydrating the peas yourself, one (1.4-ounce) package freeze-dried green peas (such as Mountain House brand), available online or from an outfitter

Gather and pack the cooking equipment you'll need for the trail:

Backpacking cook pot with lid (about 2-quart capacity)

Cook stove, adequate for securely holding the pot, and windscreen

Fuel appropriate for your stove, enough for simmering for about 10 minutes

Matches or lighter for the stove

Short wooden spoon for stirring

Short serving ladle

Mess kit for each Scout (plate and utensils)

Small cleaning pad, a few drops of biodegradable soap, and small drying towel

Hand sanitizer

The recipe also requires 2½ cups pure, filtered water to prepare on the trail. Either carry from home or, better yet, find the necessary water source along the trail.

If doing the drying yourself with a dehydrator, simply spread the fresh or frozen peas on a clean drying tray, place the tray back into the appliance, and set the dehydrator to a temperature of about 125°F. Required drying time depends on the characteristics of your appliance, but the peas should be fully dry within about 9 hours.

Package the dried peas, along with the rice and seasoning mix from the box, in a quart-size ziplock freezer bag then tightly seal. The chicken remains in its sealed pouch and is carried separately. Pack the food and gear into your backpack for the trail.

You're on the trail and it's time to eat, so now comes the fun part. Prepare your cooking zone by placing the stove in a fire-safe area away from the main foot traffic. Bare earth or the top of a large, flat rock is ideal; the cooking surface must be durable. Cook well away from combustibles such as dry grass and trees. Be sure to follow any local regulations regarding the use of open fire.

With oversight from a senior Scout or leader, set up the stove. Perform a safety check, and be sure no fuel is leaking. Once certain that the stove is in good repair, fire it up. Add 2½ cups of water to the pot then carefully set it on the stove. Be certain that the pot is centered and stable. Bring the water to a boil over high flame; while the water heats, sanitize your hands.

Add rice and pea mix followed by the chicken, then reduce flame to a simmer or very gentle boil. Stir well. If your stove won't adjust low enough to permit a gentle boil, then use the lowest heat setting that your stove permits, being certain to stir more often to prevent the food from burning. When stirring, brace the pot with your other hand to prevent the pot from tipping off the stove, using a folded cloth if necessary to protect your hand against hot metal.

The rice and peas should be fully cooked and rehydrated after about 10 minutes. If they remain a little crunchy, which may be the case when using dehydrated instead of freeze-dried peas, extend the cooking time until fully softened. Extinguish the stove and allow it to cool before moving it.

Congratulations! You've prepared your first camp backpacking recipe. Enjoy your meal.

Try to finish all of the food, if possible, to minimize food scraps to pack out. Once finished with your meal, promptly proceed with cleaning the cook gear. If food adheres stubbornly to the pot, let it soak for a few minutes in a small amount of water to loosen.

Clean water is a precious resource in the wilderness, so use just enough water and detergent to do the job. Clean your gear, being careful to bury any food scraps and waste water in a cat hole several inches deep and at least 200 feet from the nearest water source. Spotless equipment is not only hygienic but also of little interest to nosy animals looking for easy food.

Cooking rice and chicken on the trail.
DAVID LATTNER

Repack your gear for your next destination, and don't forget to pack out all the trash.

The recipe for **Rayado Rice and Chicken** comes from Emery Corley, Assistant Scoutmaster of Troop 809 in Saint Louis, Missouri. He is past director of Fish Camp on the Rayado River at Philmont Scout Ranch.

Yogi Berry Granola

¼ cup canola oil

1 (18-ounce) jar Smucker's Blackberry Jelly

2 cups lightly salted cashews, chopped

1 (16-ounce) bag Bob's Red Mill 5-Grain Rolled Hot Cereal

1 cup shredded sweetened coconut

1 ounce dried blueberries

1 ounce dried strawberries

1 ounce dried blackberries

Options: Granola can also be eaten like regular cereal using cold reconstituted milk, or it can be served warm by heating the water before reconstituting the milk powder.

PREPARATION AT HOME:

1. In a cook pot, heat canola oil and jelly until thin.
2. Add cashews to pot along with the cereal and coconut. Stir until liquid has covered the mixture evenly.
3. Spread cereal mixture in a nonstick jelly roll pan.
4. Bake at 225°F for 2 hours. Stir granola periodically to prevent uneven baking.
5. Allow granola to cool then add dried fruit and stir.
6. Store in large ziplock bags for the trail.

PREPARATION ON THE TRAIL:

1. Eat straight from the bag or serve with optional reconstituted milk.

REQUIRED EQUIPMENT ON THE TRAIL:

None

Tim Conners, Statesboro, Georgia
Assistant Scoutmaster
Troop 340, Coastal Empire Council

Christine Conners, Statesboro, Georgia
Committee Member and Merit Badge Counselor
Troop 340, Coastal Empire Council

Servings: 12 (1 cup per serving)
Total Weight: 2 pounds 9 ounces
Weight per Serving: about 3 ounces
Preparation Time on the Trail: None
Challenge Level: Easy

Johnny Appleseed Granola

¼ cup canola oil

1 (18-ounce) jar apple jelly

1 (16-ounce) bag Bob's Red Mill 5-Grain Rolled Hot Cereal

1½ cups (6 ounces) pecan pieces

1 cup shredded sweetened coconut

5 ounces dried apple rings, chopped

PREPARATION AT HOME:

1. In a cook pot, heat canola oil and apple jelly until thin.
2. Add cereal, pecans, and coconut. Stir until liquid has covered the mixture evenly.
3. Spread granola in a nonstick jelly roll pan.
4. Bake at 225°F for 2 hours. Stir granola periodically to prevent uneven baking.
5. Allow granola to cool then add chopped apples and stir.
6. Store in large ziplock bags for the trail.

PREPARATION ON THE TRAIL:

1. Eat straight from the bag or serve with optional reconstituted milk.

REQUIRED EQUIPMENT ON THE TRAIL:

None

Options: Granola can also be eaten like regular cereal using cold reconstituted milk, or it can be served warm by heating the water before reconstituting the milk powder.

Tim Conners, Statesboro, Georgia
Assistant Scoutmaster
Troop 340, Coastal Empire Council

Christine Conners, Statesboro, Georgia
Committee Member and Merit Badge Counselor
Troop 340, Coastal Empire Council

Servings: 10 (1 cup per serving)
Total Weight: 2½ pounds
Weight per Serving: 4 ounces
Preparation Time on the Trail: None
Challenge Level: Easy

Wave Rider Granola

¼ cup canola oil

1 (12-ounce) jar Smucker's pineapple preserves

1 cup lightly salted chopped macadamia nuts

1 (16-ounce) bag Bob's Red Mill 5-Grain Rolled Hot Cereal

½ cup shredded sweetened coconut

6 ounces dried mango slices, chopped

Options: Granola can also be eaten like regular cereal using cold reconstituted milk, or it can be served warm by heating the water before reconstituting the milk powder.

Servings: 7 (1 cup per serving)
Total Weight: 2 pounds 6 ounces
Weight per Serving: About 5 ounces
Preparation Time on the Trail: None
Challenge Level: Easy

PREPARATION AT HOME:

1. In a cook pot, heat oil and preserves until thin.
2. Add macadamia nuts to pot along with the cereal and coconut. Stir until liquid has covered the mixture evenly.
3. Spread cereal mixture in a nonstick jelly roll pan.
4. Bake at 250°F for 1½ hours. Stir periodically.
5. Allow granola to cool then add mango pieces and stir.
6. Store in large ziplock bags for the trail.

PREPARATION ON THE TRAIL:

1. Eat straight from the bag or serve with optional reconstituted milk.

REQUIRED EQUIPMENT ON THE TRAIL:

None

Tim Conners, Statesboro, Georgia
Assistant Scoutmaster
Troop 340, Coastal Empire Council

Christine Conners, Statesboro, Georgia
Committee Member and Merit Badge Counselor
Troop 340, Coastal Empire Council

Chocolate Banana Nut Crunch Cereal

"This is a quick and easy breakfast when you need to hit the trail running. It also makes a quickie lunch if you're getting tired of gorp and trail snacks."

1 cup Kashi GOLEAN cereal

¼ cup dried banana chips

3 tablespoons crushed walnuts

3 tablespoons Nestle Nido whole milk powder

2 tablespoons hot cocoa powder or chocolate protein powder

1 cup water, added on the trail

PREPARATION AT HOME:

1. Combine all dry ingredients in a quart-size heavy-duty ziplock bag.

PREPARATION ON THE TRAIL:

1. Add 1 cup cold water to the ziplock bag.
2. Seal and shake well.
3. Serve straight from the bag.

REQUIRED EQUIPMENT ON THE TRAIL:

None

Rob Petz, Rockton, Illinois
Scoutmaster
Troop 619, Glacier's Edge Council

TIPS: Just Bananas brand freeze-dried banana slices are a great choice for this recipe. Low-fat powdered milk can be substituted for the Nido.

Servings: 1
Total Weight: 5 ounces
Preparation Time on the Trail: 5 minutes
Challenge Level: Easy

Adirondack Apricot Oatmeal

¾ cup quick oats

1 teaspoon brown sugar or maple sugar

1 pinch salt

⅓ cup nonfat milk powder

2 apricots, dried and chopped

3 tablespoons cashew nut pieces

1½ cups water, added on the trail

PREPARATION AT HOME:

1. Package all dry ingredients in a small ziplock bag.

PREPARATION ON THE TRAIL:

1. Bring 1½ cups of water to boiling. Add oatmeal mix and stir.
2. Remove from heat and let stand for 5 minutes before serving.

REQUIRED EQUIPMENT ON THE TRAIL:

Cook pot

Ken Harbison, Rochester, New York
Former Boy Scout and Master Tester for *The Scout's Outdoor Cookbook*
Washington Trail Council

Rise and shine! It's time to eat! SCOTT H. SIMERLY SR.

Servings: 2
Total Weight: 4 ounces
Weight per Serving: 2 ounces
Preparation Time on the Trail: ¼ hour
Challenge Level: Easy

Backpackin' Cheese Grits

½ cup quick grits

¼ teaspoon salt

⅓ cup grated Parmesan cheese

1 tablespoon Butter Buds

Optional: bacon bits

2 cups water, added on the trail

PREPARATION AT HOME:

1. Combine all dry ingredients in a small ziplock bag.

PREPARATION ON THE TRAIL:

1. Bring 2 cups water to a boil.
2. Add grit mix to water and cook for about 5 minutes or until the grits become soft.

REQUIRED EQUIPMENT ON THE TRAIL:

Cook pot

Scott Simerly, Apex, North Carolina
Scoutmaster
Troop 204, Occoneechee Council

Servings: 2–3
Total Weight: 5 ounces
Weight per Serving: About 2 ounces
Preparation Time on the Trail: ¼ hour
Challenge Level: Easy

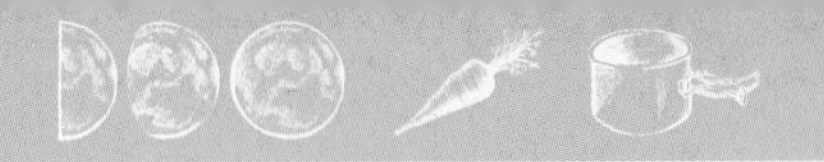

Troop 446's Apple Breakfast Cereal

- 1 45-gram packet Cream of Wheat Healthy Grain instant hot cereal
- 1 tablespoon Nestle Nido whole milk powder
- 1 tablespoon brown sugar
- 1 tablespoon dried apple pieces
- 1 tablespoon chopped walnuts
- ½ teaspoon ground cinnamon
- 1 cup water, added on the trail

PREPARATION AT HOME:

1. Combine all dry ingredients in a small ziplock bag.

PREPARATION ON THE TRAIL:

1. Bring 1 cup water to a boil and add the cereal mixture. Stir.
2. Remove from heat and allow cereal to rest for a few minutes for water to be fully absorbed before serving.

REQUIRED EQUIPMENT ON THE TRAIL:

Cook pot

Mitch Daniel, Swansboro, North Carolina
Assistant Scoutmaster
Troop 446, East Carolina Council

Servings: 1
Total Weight: 3 ounces
Preparation Time on the Trail: ¼ hour
Challenge Level: Easy

North Woods Oatmeal

¾ cup quick oats

1 teaspoon brown sugar

1 pinch salt

⅓ cup nonfat milk powder

2 tablespoons dried blueberries

1 (2-bar) package Oats 'N Honey Nature Valley Granola

1½ cups water, added on the trail

PREPARATION AT HOME:

1. Combine oats, sugar, salt, milk powder, and dried blueberries in a small ziplock bag.
2. Carry granola bars separately.

PREPARATION ON THE TRAIL:

1. Add oat mix to 1½ cups boiling water and stir.
2. Remove from heat and let stand for 5 minutes. Stir.
3. Crumble two granola bars and sprinkle on top before serving.

REQUIRED EQUIPMENT ON THE TRAIL:
Cook pot

Ken Harbison, Rochester, New York
Former Boy Scout and Master Tester for *The Scout's Outdoor Cookbook*
Washington Trail Council

Servings: 2
Total Weight: 5 ounces
Weight per Serving: About 3 ounces
Preparation Time on the Trail: ¼ hour
Challenge Level: Easy

Cheesy Potato Omelet

½ cup whole egg powder

1 (4.2-ounce) package Hungry Jack dried hash browns

¼ cup dried cheese powder

2 tablespoons dried minced onion

¼ cup bacon bits

Optional: 2 tablespoons dried bell pepper

Salt and pepper to taste

3 cups water, added on the trail, plus additional for BakePacker

"This recipe was created during a warm-up backpacking trip along the Chesapeake and Ohio Canal. Our older Scouts were practicing their cooking techniques and developing trekking skills needed for an upcoming high-adventure week in West Virginia."

PREPARATION AT HOME:

1. Combine egg powder, dried hash browns, cheese powder, dried onion, bacon bits, and optional dried bell pepper in a quart-size ziplock bag.
2. Carry salt and pepper separately.

PREPARATION ON THE TRAIL:

1. Place pack oven into pot large enough to accommodate the standard-size BakePacker. Fill pot to top of BakePacker grid with water.
2. Pour dried ingredients along with 3 cups water into oven bag and mix thoroughly by kneading.
3. Set bag on top of BakePacker grid. Spread bag out on the grid and fold the top over loosely. Cover the pot with a lid.
4. Bring water to a boil for 18 minutes.
5. Carefully serve omelet from the bag.

REQUIRED EQUIPMENT ON THE TRAIL:

4-quart cook pot with lid
Standard-size (7⅜-inch) BakePacker
Large-size (not "turkey-size") oven bag

Linda Nosalik, Upper Marlboro, Maryland
Assistant Scoutmaster and Venture Patrol Adviser
Troop 1575, National Capital Area Council

Servings: 3–4
Total Weight: 10 ounces
Weight per Serving: About 3 ounces
Preparation Time on the Trail: ½ hour
Challenge Level: Easy

Best Oatmeal Ever!

"This recipe is so good, we even make it at home. It also helps us get over the winter slump when we can't get outdoors as often as we'd like because we're buried in snow. 'Be prepared' . . . to share some once the other Scouts get a whiff."

½ cup quick oats

¼ cup Craisins

3 tablespoons Nestle Nido whole milk powder

2 tablespoons slivered almonds

1 tablespoon granulated sugar

Ground cinnamon to taste

1 cup water, added on trail

PREPARATION AT HOME:

1. Combine all dry ingredients in a small ziplock bag.

PREPARATION ON THE TRAIL:

1. Bring 1 cup water to a boil and add the oat mixture. Stir to eliminate clumps.
2. Remove from heat and allow oatmeal to rest for a few minutes for water to be absorbed and for oats to soften before serving.

REQUIRED EQUIPMENT ON THE TRAIL:

Cook pot

Rob Petz, Rockton, Illinois
Scoutmaster
Troop 619, Glacier's Edge Council

Servings: 1
Total Weight: 5 ounces
Preparation Time on the Trail: ¼ hour
Challenge Level: Easy

Ketchikan Couscous

⅓ cup Fantastic Foods whole-wheat couscous

2 tablespoons nonfat milk powder

2 tablespoons chopped dates or dried fruit of your choice

½ tablespoon brown sugar

1 pinch salt

1 dash ground cinnamon

2 tablespoons chopped walnuts or nuts of your choice

⅔ cup water, added on trail

Options: Real butter or Butter Buds can be added for a creamier flavor.

PREPARATION AT HOME:

1. Combine all dry ingredients and package in a ziplock bag for the trail.

PREPARATION ON THE TRAIL:

1. Heat ⅔ cup water to boiling.
2. Stir in couscous mix and cook for 2 minutes. Remove from heat.
3. Allow the pot to stand covered until liquid is absorbed and the couscous becomes tender, about 5 minutes.

REQUIRED EQUIPMENT ON THE TRAIL:

Cook pot

Ken Harbison, Rochester, New York
Former Boy Scout and Master Tester for *The Scout's Outdoor Cookbook*
Washington Trail Council

The "green tunnel" along the Appalachian Trail.
TIM CONNERS

Servings: 1
Total Weight: 5 ounces
Preparation Time on the Trail: ¼ hour
Challenge Level: Easy

Chuckwalla Chocolate Chip Pancakes

⅔ cup Aunt Jemima or Hungry Jack pancake mix

2 tablespoons mini chocolate chips or chopped regular chips

3 tablespoons maple or pancake syrup

1 teaspoon vegetable oil, plus extra for contingency

½ cup water, added on trail

PREPARATION AT HOME:

1. Place pancake mix and chocolate chips into a quart-size heavy-duty ziplock bag.
2. Carry syrup and vegetable oil separately.

PREPARATION ON THE TRAIL:

1. Add ½ cup cold water to dry ingredients in the ziplock bag.
2. Knead mixture well enough to break up the larger lumps. Do not overwork the batter as this will make the pancakes less tender.
3. Grease pan with 1 teaspoon vegetable oil.
4. Warm the pan over medium heat until drops of water sizzle and disappear quickly.
5. Pour or spoon approximately ¼ of the batter at a time into the heated pan, flipping once bubbles begin to form in batter.
6. Add additional oil to the skillet, if needed, for subsequent pancakes.
7. Serve with syrup.

REQUIRED EQUIPMENT ON THE TRAIL:

Skillet
Spatula

Ken Harbison, Rochester, New York
Former Boy Scout and Master Tester for *The Scout's Outdoor Cookbook*
Washington Trail Council

Servings: 1
Total Weight: 6 ounces
Preparation Time on the Trail: ½ hour
Challenge Level: Moderate

Arapaho Apple Pancakes

1½ cups Arrowhead Mills Multigrain Pancake and Waffle mix

3 ounces dried apple rings, finely chopped

1 (1-serving) packet spiced apple cider mix

2 tablespoons vegetable oil

½ cup water per serving, added on the trail

PREPARATION AT HOME:

1. In a bowl, combine pancake mix, apple pieces, and apple cider mix.
2. Divide mixture evenly between two quart-size heavy-duty ziplock bags.
3. Package oil separately for the trail.

PREPARATION ON THE TRAIL:

1. To prepare 1 serving, warm 1 tablespoon oil in frying pan over low heat.
2. To 1 bag add ½ cup water. Knead mixture by breaking apart large clumps.
3. Cut a corner from the bottom of bag and squeeze enough batter into the pan to make 1 pancake.
4. Flip the pancake once it is browned on the bottom. Brown the other side and serve.
5. Repeat for the remainder of the batter.

REQUIRED EQUIPMENT ON THE TRAIL:

Skillet
Spatula

Tim Conners, Statesboro, Georgia
Assistant Scoutmaster
Troop 340, Coastal Empire Council

Christine Conners, Statesboro, Georgia
Committee Member and Merit Badge Counselor
Troop 340, Coastal Empire Council

Servings: 2
Total Weight: 15 ounces
Weight per Serving: About 7 ounces
Preparation Time on the Trail: ½ hour
Challenge Level: Moderate

Patrol Pineapple Pancakes

1 (20-ounce) can Dole crushed pineapple in syrup

1½ cups Arrowhead Mills Multigrain Pancake and Waffle mix

1 tablespoon vegetable oil

Optional: Syrup or powdered sugar

⅔ cup water per serving, added on the trail

PREPARATION AT HOME:

1. Dry pineapple along with its juice on a plastic or parchment-lined dehydrating tray.
2. Divide dried pineapple evenly between 2 quart-size heavy-duty ziplock bags.
3. Add ¾ cup pancake mix to each bag and seal.
4. Carry vegetable oil and optional syrup or powdered sugar separately.

PREPARATION ON THE TRAIL:

1. To prepare 1 serving, add ⅔ cup water to 1 bag of pineapple pancake mix. Knead the bag to eliminate large chunks from the batter.
2. Wait about 20 minutes, giving the pineapple time to rehydrate.
3. Heat ½ tablespoon vegetable oil in a pan.
4. Cut corner from bottom of the ziplock bag and squeeze batter into pan.
5. Cook as for regular pancakes, flipping immediately once bubbles begin to form in the batter then briefly finishing on the second side.

REQUIRED EQUIPMENT ON THE TRAIL:

Skillet
Spatula

Tim Conners, Statesboro, Georgia
Assistant Scoutmaster
Troop 340, Coastal Empire Council

Christine Conners, Statesboro, Georgia
Committee Member and Merit Badge Counselor
Troop 340, Coastal Empire Council

Servings: 2
Total Weight: 13 ounces
Weight per Serving: About 7 ounces
Preparation Time on the Trail: ¾ hour
Challenge Level: Moderate

Pancake and Bacon Sandwich

1 (16.4-ounce, 12-count) package frozen Eggo buttermilk pancakes

1 (2-ounce, 12-count) package precooked bacon

6 individual condiment packets honey, about 2 ounces total

Optional: 2 tablespoons butter

Option: Pancake sandwiches can be warmed, if desired, by placing them in an oven bag then setting the bag directly above or in boiling water.

Caution: Butter can be left unrefrigerated for 1 or 2 days, but after that, it will spoil rapidly.

Servings: 6
Total Weight: 1 pound 6 ounces
Weight per Serving: About 4 ounces
Preparation Time on the Trail: ¼ hour
Challenge Level: Easy

PREPARATION AT HOME:

1. Remove pancakes and precooked bacon from their packages, but retain the pancakes and bacon in their original sealed plastic bags for the trail.
2. Carry honey and optional butter separately.

PREPARATION ON THE TRAIL:

1. Spread optional butter on 6 pancakes.
2. Cut each bacon slice in half and place 4 halves on each of the buttered pancakes.
3. Cover bacon slices with honey and set another pancake on top to make 6 sandwiches.

REQUIRED EQUIPMENT ON THE TRAIL:

None

John Malachowski, Stewartstown, Pennsylvania
Scoutmaster
Troop 27, The New Birth of Freedom Council

Bacon and Peanut Butter Bagel

1 (2-ounce, 12-count) package precooked bacon

1 (22-ounce, 6-count) package plain bagels

6 tablespoons peanut butter

PREPARATION AT HOME:

1. Remove precooked bacon from its outer package, but retain in its original sealed plastic bag for the trail.
2. Remove bagels from their bag. Split bagels and spread ½ tablespoon peanut butter on each half.
3. Return bagels to their original bag and pack for the trail.

PREPARATION ON THE TRAIL:

1. Cut each bacon slice in half and place 4 halves in each of the bagel sandwiches.

REQUIRED EQUIPMENT ON THE TRAIL:

None

Option: Bagel sandwiches can be warmed, if desired, by placing them in an oven bag then setting the bag directly above or in boiling water.

John Malachowski, Stewartstown, Pennsylvania
Scoutmaster
Troop 27, The New Birth of Freedom Council

Servings: 6
Total Weight: 1¾ pounds
Weight per Serving: About 5 ounces
Preparation Time on the Trail: 5 minutes
Challenge Level: Easy

Camel Rider Omelet

2 tablespoons whole egg powder

¼ cup real bacon bits

¼ cup grated Parmesan cheese

2 tablespoons dried onion flakes

⅛ teaspoon ground black pepper

1 tablespoon McCormick Perfect Pinch roasted garlic and bell pepper

Optional: 2 tablespoons dried bell peppers

1 pita bread

⅔ cup water, added on the trail

"'Camel Rider' is a common name for a pita sandwich in the South. Most any mom-and-pop sandwich shop has the camel rider on their breakfast menu."

PREPARATION AT HOME:

1. Place all dry ingredients, except for pita, into a quart-size ziplock bag.
2. Carry pita bread separately.

PREPARATION AT CAMP:

1. In a pot, bring ⅔ cup water to a boil.
2. Add egg mixture and stir until water is fully absorbed. Remove from heat.
3. Slice pita in half and transfer cooked egg mix to the pocket.

REQUIRED EQUIPMENT ON THE TRAIL:

Cook pot

Jason Cagle, Jacksonville, Florida
Assistant Scoutmaster
Troop 169, North Florida Council

Servings: 1
Total Weight: About 5 ounces
Preparation Time on the Trail: ¼ hour
Challenge Level: Easy

Bacon and Egg Bagel

"Bagels are an ideal bread for backpackers. They don't crush easily, and who knows if they ever go stale."

1 (2-ounce, 12-count) package precooked bacon

1 (22-ounce, 6-count) package plain bagels, sliced

2 tablespoons butter, softened

Scrambled Egg Mix:

1½ cups whole egg powder

½ teaspoon salt

½ teaspoon ground black pepper

1 teaspoon garlic powder

2 tablespoons dried chives

4 teaspoons Butter Buds

2 tablespoons vegetable oil

2¼ cups water, added on the trail

PREPARATION AT HOME:

1. Remove precooked bacon from its package but retain it in the original sealed plastic bag for the trail.
2. Remove bagels from their bag. Split bagels and spread butter on each half.
3. Return bagels to their original bag and pack them for the trail.
4. Prepare scrambled egg mix by combining egg powder, salt, black pepper, garlic powder, chives, and Butter Buds in a quart-size heavy-duty ziplock bag.
5. Carry vegetable oil separately.

PREPARATION ON THE TRAIL:

1. Add 2¼ cups water to scrambled egg mix in ziplock bag and knead out the clumps.
2. Heat oil in skillet over medium heat and pour eggs from ziplock bag into pan. Cook eggs in batches if the pan is small.
3. Scramble eggs until they congeal.
4. Break each bacon slice in half and place 4 pieces on each of 6 bagel halves.
5. Spoon eggs over bacon slices on the bagel halves, then cover each with another bagel half to make 6 sandwiches.

REQUIRED EQUIPMENT ON THE TRAIL:
Skillet

John Malachowski, Stewartstown, Pennsylvania
Scoutmaster
Troop 27, The New Birth of Freedom Council

Option: Bagel sandwiches can be warmed, if desired, by placing them in an oven bag then setting the bag directly above or in boiling water.

Caution: Butter can be left unrefrigerated for 1 or 2 days, but after that, it will spoil rapidly.

Servings: 6
Total Weight: 2 pounds 2 ounces
Weight per Serving: About 6 ounces
Preparation Time on the Trail: ½ hour
Challenge Level: Moderate

Yosemite Yogurt Drops

1 (6-ounce) container vanilla or blended-fruit yogurt

Options: Yogurt can also be dried as a single sheet of "leather."

Create your own inventions by pureeing fresh fruit and plain yogurt together or adding flavor extracts or candy sprinkles to the yogurt before drying.

PREPARATION AT HOME:

1. Scoop tablespoon-size yogurt drops onto a lined dehydrator tray.
2. Dry until the yogurt is firm and leathery.
3. Package into a small ziplock bag for the trail.

REQUIRED EQUIPMENT ON THE TRAIL:
None

Tim Conners, Statesboro, Georgia
Assistant Scoutmaster
Troop 340, Coastal Empire Council

Christine Conners, Statesboro, Georgia
Committee Member and Merit Badge Counselor
Troop 340, Coastal Empire Council

Servings: 1
Total Weight: Less than 1 ounce
Preparation Time on the Trail: None
Challenge Level: Easy

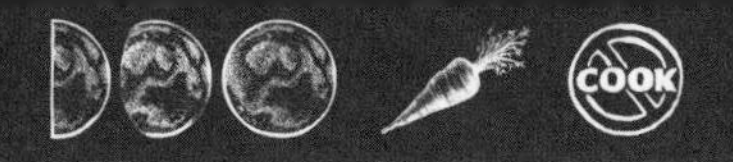

Northville-Placid Trail Balls

½ cup peanut butter

½ cup honey

1 cup nonfat milk powder

1 cup Quaker Old Fashioned oats

¼ cup toasted wheat germ

PREPARATION AT HOME:

1. Stir together peanut butter and honey.
2. Add milk powder and oatmeal.
3. Thoroughly mix then shape into approximately 2 dozen balls.
4. Roll each piece in wheat germ then let stand several hours before packaging.
5. Wrap individually in wax paper or plastic then store in a ziplock bag or plastic container for the trail.

REQUIRED EQUIPMENT ON THE TRAIL:

None

Sherry Bennett, Rochester, New York
Former Den Leader and Merit Badge Counselor
Otetiana Council

Servings: 24 (1 ball per serving)
Total Weight: 1 pound
Weight per Serving: Less than 1 ounce
Preparation Time on the Trail: None
Challenge Level: Easy

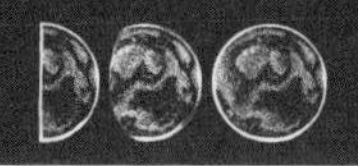

Barterer's Cheese Coins

2 cups finely grated sharp cheddar cheese

½ cup butter, softened

½ tablespoon Worcestershire sauce

1 tablespoon sesame seeds

1 cup all-purpose flour

"If food can be considered a form of currency on the trail, then these 'coins' have the value of gold."

PREPARATION AT HOME:

1. Combine cheese, butter, Worcestershire sauce, and sesame seeds in a bowl.
2. Add flour a little at a time while kneading.
3. Form dough into a long roll about 1 inch in diameter.
4. Cut roll into ¼-inch-thick slices.
5. Bake coins at 350°F for about 15 minutes.
6. Let cool then package for the trail.

REQUIRED EQUIPMENT ON THE TRAIL:

None

Sherry Bennett, Rochester, New York
Former Den Leader and Merit Badge Counselor
Otetiana Council

Servings: About 15 (4 "coins" per serving)
Total Weight: 15 ounces
Weight per Serving: 1 ounce
Preparation Time on the Trail: None
Challenge Level: Easy

Niagara Falls Bars

2⅔ cups Quaker Old Fashioned oats

½ cup plus 1 tablespoon whole-wheat flour

6 tablespoons all-purpose flour

½ cup sesame seeds

½ cup brown sugar

¼ teaspoon ground cinnamon

1½ teaspoons salt

⅓ cup nonfat milk powder

½ cup vegetable oil

¾ cup honey

2 teaspoons vanilla extract

PREPARATION AT HOME:

1. Preheat oven to 325°F.
2. Mix all dry ingredients together in a large bowl.
3. Heat oil, honey, and vanilla extract in a pan then add to dry ingredients in the bowl. Mix well.
4. Pat batter into a 9 x 13-inch parchment-lined pan.
5. Bake for 30 minutes.
6. Cool then slice into 32 bars.
7. Seal in plastic food wrap for the trail.

REQUIRED EQUIPMENT ON THE TRAIL:
None

Sherry Bennett, Rochester, New York
Former Den Leader and Merit Badge Counselor
Otetiana Council

Servings: 32 bars
Total Weight: 2 pounds
Weight per Serving: 1 ounce
Preparation Time on the Trail: None
Challenge Level: Easy

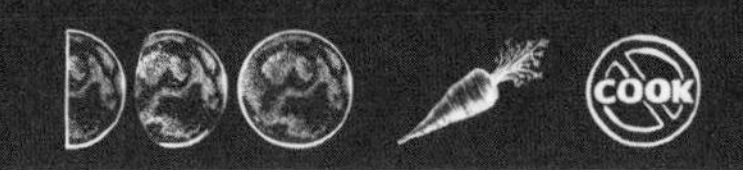

Mountain Man Bars

- 4 cups crushed cereal (see below)
- 1½ cups chopped dried fruit (see below)
- 1½ cups chopped unsalted nuts (see below)
- ¼–½ cup "extras" (see below)
- ¼ cup whole-wheat flour
- 1 teaspoon salt
- ⅔ cup honey or maple syrup
- 4 eggs
- Optional: flavor extract (see below)

Christine Conners, Statesboro, Georgia
Committee Member and Merit Badge Counselor
Troop 340, Coastal Empire Council

Tim Conners, Statesboro, Georgia
Assistant Scoutmaster
Troop 340, Coastal Empire Council

"This recipe allows a lot of customization according to your specific tastes. With the price of store-bought granola bars going through the roof, and no shortage of picky Scouts, Mountain Man Bars are a must-have for any large group trek."

PREPARATION AT HOME:

1. Preheat oven to 300°F.
2. Place a sheet of parchment paper over a 17 x 11-inch baking sheet.
3. In a large bowl, combine cereal, fruit, nuts, "extras," flour, and salt.
4. In a separate bowl, whisk together honey or syrup, eggs, and optional flavor extract.
5. Pour honey-syrup mix into the bowl with the dry ingredients and stir well.
6. Evenly spread the batter an inch or two shy of the edges of the baking sheet.
7. Bake for about 45 minutes or until dry to the touch.
8. Let cool then slice into 32 bars.

REQUIRED EQUIPMENT ON THE TRAIL:

None

Customize your bars by choosing from the following categories:

Cereal: wheat flakes, corn flakes, granola, muesli, or puffed rice

Dried Fruit: pineapple, prunes, raisins, cherries, blueberries, apricots, apples, strawberries, cranberries, dates, figs, mangos, peaches, or pears

Nuts: pine nuts, peanuts, macadamias, hazelnuts, almonds, cashews, walnuts, pistachios, or pecans

Extras: sunflower seeds, poppy seeds, sesame seeds, shredded coconut, toasted wheat germ, or chocolate chips

Flavor Extract: vanilla, almond, cinnamon, banana, cherry, strawberry, orange, raspberry, or coconut

Servings: 32 bars
Total Weight: About 2½ pounds (depending on ingredient selection)
Weight per Serving: About 1 ounce
Preparation Time on the Trail: None
Challenge Level: Easy

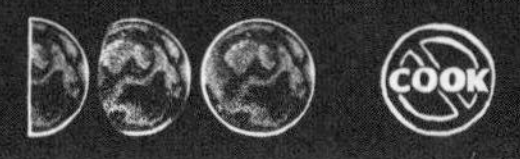

Fear-Factor Beef Jerky

"Our Scouts love homemade beef jerky. On a recent trip along the Appalachian Trail, the Conners family brought homemade jerky while some of the Scouts packed the creepy-looking, store-bought stuff. No question about it: Our jerky beat theirs hands down, not only for flavor and texture but for the lower fear factor."

1 pound flank steak

¼ cup soy sauce

¼ cup Worcestershire sauce

½ teaspoon garlic powder

½ teaspoon onion powder

½ teaspoon Liquid Smoke (your favorite flavor)

2 tablespoons maple syrup

PREPARATION AT HOME:

1. Place wrapped and thawed meat in the freezer for about an hour, or until the beef becomes semi-frozen for easier slicing.
2. In a large bowl, combine soy sauce, Worcestershire sauce, garlic powder, onion powder, Liquid Smoke, and maple syrup.
3. Slice steak into ¼-inch-thick strips, along the grain for the standard chewy texture.
4. Marinate meat in the soy sauce mixture in the refrigerator overnight.
5. Lay individual slices of meat side by side, but not touching, on an oven tray. Use a second tray if the first one becomes too crowded.
6. Set oven to 170°F. Place trays in oven, propping the door open an inch or so to provide ventilation and to prevent the oven from becoming too warm.
7. Allow jerky to dry 6 to 8 hours. It will become very dark. Once properly dried, bending should cause the meat to crack but not separate. If the jerky snaps apart when bent, the meat has become too dry. It's still quite edible, but it will be somewhat difficult to chew.
8. While the jerky is still warm, pat both sides with paper towels to remove excess grease. Standing grease will reduce the meat's shelf life.
9. To further lengthen shelf life, do not store at room temperature. Instead, refrigerate or freeze the jerky then pack for the trail in ziplock bags once ready to go.

REQUIRED EQUIPMENT ON THE TRAIL:
None

Tim Conners,
Statesboro, Georgia
Assistant Scoutmaster
Troop 340, Coastal Empire Council

Christine Conners,
Statesboro, Georgia
Committee Member and Merit Badge Counselor
Troop 340, Coastal Empire Council

Servings: 5
Total Weight: 10 ounces
Weight per Serving: 2 ounces
Preparation Time on the Trail: None
Challenge Level: Moderate

Coyote Butte Coleslaw

½ cup lemon juice

1 cup white vinegar

1½ cups granulated sugar

1 teaspoon salt

1 teaspoon ground mustard seed

1 teaspoon celery seed

1 (16-ounce) bag fresh coleslaw vegetable mix

1 carrot, shredded

1 cup chopped sweet onion

½ cup chopped bell pepper

⅔ cup water per serving, added on the trail

Option: Once on the trail, add the contents from a condiment packet of vinegar for additional tang.

"Coyote Butte is a section of the Paria Canyon-Vermilion Cliffs Wilderness in Arizona and Utah containing spectacular sandstone formations known as 'The Wave.' Because of the fragile nature of the formations, permits are granted for only twenty people per day."

PREPARATION AT HOME:

1. Heat lemon juice, vinegar, sugar, salt, mustard seed, and celery seed, stirring to dissolve the sugar. Immediately remove from heat once the syrupy mixture reaches boiling.
2. Combine the coleslaw mix, carrot, onion, and bell pepper in a bowl and cover with the hot vinegar syrup.
3. Refrigerate, covered, for at least 8 hours, mixing at least once during the period.
4. Drain then spread the vegetable mixture thinly and evenly onto parchment or plastic-lined dehydrator trays.
5. Dry, breaking up any clumps part-way through the drying process.
6. Once dry, distribute the slaw mixture evenly between 4 heavy-duty quart-size ziplock bags.

PREPARATION ON THE TRAIL:

1. To prepare 1 serving, add ⅔ cup water to 1 bag of slaw.
2. Allow to rehydrate for at least 30 minutes before serving.

REQUIRED EQUIPMENT ON THE TRAIL:

None

Ken Harbison, Rochester, New York
Former Boy Scout and Master Tester for *The Scout's Outdoor Cookbook*
Washington Trail Council

Servings: 4
Total Weight: 7 ounces
Weight per Serving: About 2 ounces
Preparation Time on the Trail: ½ hour
Challenge Level: Easy

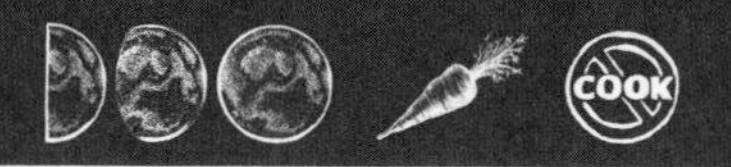

Rodman Dam Hydro Sludge

"I've heard of gorp recipes and tried a few. Most were too bland for my taste. So, for my troop's 20-miler at Rodman Dam in Florida, I invented my own energy fuel. This recipe is full of carbs and protein for backpacking. It can be eaten for lunch, a snack, or for breakfast on the trail."

3 heaping tablespoons chunky peanut butter

2 tablespoons maple syrup

½ cup corn flakes or toasted rice cereal

¼ cup raisins

PREPARATION AT HOME:

1. In a small bowl, blend all ingredients together.
2. Spoon sludge into a small ziplock bag then place this bag inside a second bag.

PREPARATION ON THE TRAIL:

1. When ready to eat, cut a large corner from the sludge bag and squeeze into mouth.
2. Store leftovers and trash inside the second unopened bag.

REQUIRED EQUIPMENT ON THE TRAIL:

None

Jason Cagle, Jacksonville, Florida
Assistant Scoutmaster
Troop 169, North Florida Council

Servings: 1
Total Weight: 5 ounces
Preparation Time on Trail: None
Challenge Level: Easy

Surfer's Gorp

6 ounces dried mango, torn into bite-size pieces

8 ounces chopped dates

6 ounces dried pineapple pieces

1 cup sweetened shredded coconut

2 cups roasted and salted macadamia nuts

PREPARATION AT HOME:

1. Combine ingredients together. Mix well.
2. Package 1 cup gorp into each of seven 1-quart-size ziplock bags, or carry it all in a 1-gallon-size bag.

REQUIRED EQUIPMENT ON THE TRAIL:

None

Tim Conners, Statesboro, Georgia
Assistant Scoutmaster
Troop 340, Coastal Empire Council

Christine Conners, Statesboro, Georgia
Committee Member and Merit Badge Counselor
Troop 340, Coastal Empire Council

Servings: 7 (1 cup per serving)
Total Weight: 2 pounds 3 ounces
Weight per Serving: 5 ounces
Preparation Time on the Trail: None
Challenge Level: Easy

Fresh greens on the trail? Absolutely! A sprout bag makes it easy. *CHRISTINE CONNERS*

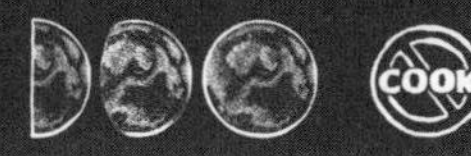

Good Ol' Raisins and Peanuts

"Gorp is one of the 'essentials' for any backpacking trip. Giving each Scout their own gorp bag allows them to refuel their body as needed without having to stop and dig through the packs of others. This is a core gorp recipe, but the variations are limitless. I take extra along on all our hikes so that the Scouts who didn't bring anything to snack on always have a reasonably healthy, energy-building option."

PREPARATION AT HOME:

1. Combine ingredients in a large bowl.
2. Divide equally into ziplock bags for individual servings.

REQUIRED EQUIPMENT ON THE TRAIL:

None

Darrick Bria, Schaumburg, Illinois
Assistant Scoutmaster
Troop 196, Northwest Suburban Council

1 pound dry-roasted peanuts

1 (15-ounce) container raisins

1 (19-ounce) bag milk chocolate M&Ms

Options to add to taste:

Dates
Dried pineapple
Dried pears
Dried apricots
Crumbled granola bars
Coconut flakes
Sunflower seeds
Pine nuts
Cashews
Walnuts
Pecans
Soy nuts

TIP: Have each Scout write their name on their bag. Otherwise, during the chaos of breaks on the trail or during camp setup or breakdown, the gorp bags are bound to become mixed up.

Servings: 9
Total Weight: 3 pounds 2 ounces (without additional options)
Weight per Serving: About 6 ounces
Preparation Time on the Trail: None
Challenge Level: Easy

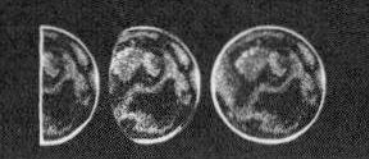

High Sierra Peanut Butter and Honey Roll-Ups

3 tablespoons peanut butter, softened

2 tablespoons honey

1 burrito-size flour tortilla

Options: Your favorite jelly can be substituted for the honey. A healthier option can be had by using natural peanut butter and a whole-wheat tortilla.

PREPARATION AT HOME:

1. Combine peanut butter and honey in a quart-size heavy-duty ziplock bag.
2. Carry tortilla separately.

PREPARATION ON THE TRAIL:

1. Cut a corner from the bottom of the ziplock bag and squirt contents into the tortilla.
2. Roll like a burrito before serving.

REQUIRED EQUIPMENT ON THE TRAIL:

None

Tim Conners, Statesboro, Georgia
Assistant Scoutmaster
Troop 340, Coastal Empire Council

Christine Conners, Statesboro, Georgia
Committee Member and Merit Badge Counselor
Troop 340, Coastal Empire Council

Servings: 1
Total Weight: About 6 ounces
Preparation Time on the Trail: 5 minutes
Challenge Level: Easy

Tehachapi Trail Sprouts

"Growing sprouts on a long trek is a great way to enjoy fresh, healthy greens when your body is craving them at a time when they would otherwise be impossible to come by. It's also a fun project for the Scouts, clean and easy to do using a sprout bag."

2 tablespoons sprout seeds: alfalfa, red clover, chia, mung, green pea, fenugreek, mustard, radish, bean mix, lentil, garbanzo, rye, hard or soft wheat, red pea, or barley

PREPARATION ON THE TRAIL:

1. Soak seeds in a little water inside a ziplock bag for 8 to 10 hours (this can also be done at home before leaving for the trail).
2. Place seeds in sprout bag and soak the bag in water for several minutes.
3. Close sprout bag and place it in a second bag, one reasonably waterproof such as a dry sack, then hang it from your pack. Don't seal the bag tightly shut because the seeds need fresh air.
4. At least twice each day, such as when stopping to fill your water bottles, remove the seed bag from the waterproof bag, and pour some filtered water over the seed bag to keep it fresh and moist. Massage the seeds very gently through the wall of the seed bag to help keep the air circulating before returning the seed bag to the waterproof bag.
5. Most varieties of grains and beans will be fully sprouted and ready to eat in 3 to 6 days.

REQUIRED EQUIPMENT ON THE TRAIL:

Sprout bag (see Tips) and dry sack

TIPS:

- A variety of "sprout bag" material can be used to grow sprouts, including cheesecloth, muslin, hosiery socks, ring-less aquarium filter bags, gauze, or even mosquito netting.
- Extreme outdoor temperatures, hot or cold, will affect the sprouting performance.
- Be sure to keep the sprouts continuously moist.
- To add deeper green to your sprouts, expose them periodically to indirect sunlight.

Tim Conners, Statesboro, Georgia
Assistant Scoutmaster
Troop 340, Coastal Empire Council

Christine Conners, Statesboro, Georgia
Committee Member and Merit Badge Counselor
Troop 340, Coastal Empire Council

Servings: 2–3
Total Weight: About 1 ounce plus weight of water for sprouting
Preparation Time on the Trail: 3–6 days, depending on seed type
Challenge Level: Easy

Tuna "Melt"

1 English muffin

1 (2½-ounce) foil pouch tuna

2 condiment packets mayonnaise

1 condiment packet yellow mustard

2 slices cheese (your choice)

Options: A chicken foil pouch can be substituted for the tuna pack.

A true melt can be had by warming the sandwich over heat in a covered pan.

PREPARATION AT HOME:

1. Package ingredients separately for the trail.

PREPARATION ON THE TRAIL:

1. Break English muffins into two halves.
2. Open tuna pouch and drain any excess liquid.
3. Squirt contents of mayo and mustard packets into tuna pouch then knead or stir.
4. Spoon the tuna mix on the muffin halves and add cheese slices to create a sandwich.

REQUIRED EQUIPMENT ON THE TRAIL:

None

Leslie Anderson, Harrison, Arkansas
Assistant Scoutmaster
Troop 111, Westark Area Council

TIP: Condiment packets can be purchased online. See Appendix B for sources.

Servings: 1
Total Weight: 6 ounces
Preparation Time on the Trail: 5 minutes
Challenge Level: Easy

Boston Brown Bread with Cream Cheese and Jelly

PREPARATION AT HOME:

1. Package all ingredients separately for the trail.

PREPARATION ON THE TRAIL:

1. Open both sides of the bread can then gently push the bread out.
2. Slice bread into 8 individual pieces, each about ½ inch thick.
3. Spread cheese and jelly on each pair of slices to create 4 sandwiches.

REQUIRED EQUIPMENT ON THE TRAIL:

Can opener

Ken Spiegel, Farmingville, New York
Committee Member
Troop 80, Suffolk County Council

1 (16-ounce) can B&M Original Brown Bread

4 (1-ounce) bricks Philadelphia mini cream cheese

4 tablespoons jelly (your favorite)

Option: For hot sandwiches, fry slices on each side with a little butter until lightly toasted before adding cream cheese and jelly.

Caution: Cream cheese should not be left unrefrigerated for a long period of time because of the risk of spoilage. Do not carry cream cheese on the trail if the weather will be very warm, and use any that you do carry within a day or so after taking it out of the refrigerator or cooler. Do not use if the cheese shows signs of spoilage.

Servings: 4
Total Weight: 1½ pounds
Weight per Serving: About 6 ounces
Preparation Time on the Trail: ¼ hour
Challenge Level: Easy

Three Sisters Salsa

1 pound salsa (your favorite)

1 cup water, added on the trail

"Salsa is easy to dry, even easier to rehydrate, and makes a wonderful accompaniment on the trail. This recipe is a great example of the world of culinary variety a dehydrator opens for the backpacker."

PREPARATION AT HOME:

1. Pour salsa on a lined dehydrator tray. Spread thinly.
2. Dry salsa to a leather then tear into pieces and store in a quart-size heavy-duty ziplock bag for the trail.

PREPARATION ON THE TRAIL:

1. Add 1 cup of water to the bag of salsa. Seal and knead bag for several minutes.
2. Allow salsa to rest until fully rehydrated.
3. Serve with trail-tough breads, crackers, or your favorite dishes.

REQUIRED EQUIPMENT ON THE TRAIL:

None

Tim Conners, Statesboro, Georgia
Assistant Scoutmaster
Troop 340, Coastal Empire Council

Christine Conners, Statesboro, Georgia
Committee Member and Merit Badge Counselor
Troop 340, Coastal Empire Council

Servings: 2–3
Total Weight: 2 ounces
Weight per Serving: About 1 ounce
Preparation Time on the Trail: ½ hour
Challenge Level: Easy

Great Lakes Ground Beef

"This is a common method for dehydrating ground meats. Once rehydrated, they can be added to a variety of dishes, including spaghetti, prepackaged rice, potatoes, and so forth."

1 pound lean ground beef or other meat

1 cup water, added on the trail

Option: Meat can also be dried on baking trays in the kitchen oven at 170°F with the door slightly ajar.

PREPARATION AT HOME:

1. In a frying pan, brown ground meat while breaking into very small pieces until fully cooked.
2. Drain grease, place meat in a colander, then rinse in hot water to remove excess fat.
3. Evenly distribute meat on a lined dehydrator tray and dry at 155°F until it becomes brittle and hard.
4. Pat any remaining grease from the meat with a paper towel.
5. Allow meat to cool then package in a quart-size heavy-duty ziplock bag along with a clean, folded paper towel.
6. Refrigerate or freeze dried meat until ready to leave for the trail. Dried ground meats are fairly durable, but to reduce risk of spoilage, plan to use within a couple of weeks after removing from the refrigerator or freezer.

PREPARATION ON THE TRAIL:

1. Add dried ground beef to 1 cup of water and bring to a boil.
2. Reduce heat, cover pot, and simmer until the water is mostly absorbed. This won't take long.
3. Once rehydrated, drain any remaining water then add meat to your favorite dishes.

REQUIRED EQUIPMENT ON THE TRAIL:

Cook pot

Tim Conners, Statesboro, Georgia
Assistant Scoutmaster
Troop 340, Coastal Empire Council

Christine Conners, Statesboro, Georgia
Committee Member and Merit Badge Counselor
Troop 340, Coastal Empire Council

Servings: 7–8
Total Weight: 4 ounces
Weight per Serving: Less than 1 ounce
Preparation Time on Trail: ¼ hour
Challenge Level: Moderate

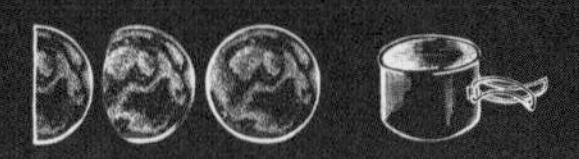

EBC Soup

1 standard cube instant chicken bouillon

2 tablespoons whole egg powder

1 tablespoon dried chives

1½ cups water, added on the trail

"Egg, bouillon, and chive soup is simple and tastes great. I like it because it is loaded in protein, is simple to make, and has a way of getting your motor running."

PREPARATION AT HOME:

1. In a small ziplock bag, combine bouillon cube, egg powder, and chives.

PREPARATION ON THE TRAIL:

1. Add egg mixture to 1½ cups water in a pot and bring to a boil.
2. Stir while breaking up egg clumps.
3. After a good boil, the egg will congeal at the top. Once it does, remove from heat and serve.

REQUIRED EQUIPMENT ON THE TRAIL:

Cook pot

Thomas Leggemann, Greensboro, North Carolina
Assistant Den Leader
Den 11, Old North State Council

Egg soup--fast and easy! *CHRISTINE CONNERS*

Servings: 1
Total Weight: About 1 ounce
Preparation Time on the Trail: ¼ hour
Challenge Level: Easy

Wonton Soup

4 ounces frozen precooked wontons (your favorite), thawed

1 (0.28-ounce) packet Dynasty wonton soup base mix

2 tablespoons dried chives

3 cups water, added on the trail

PREPARATION AT HOME:

1. Chop wontons into small pieces.
2. Place chopped wontons on a lined dehydrator tray and dry.
3. Place dried wontons in a quart-size ziplock bag.
4. Toss soup packet into the wonton bag along with the chives.

PREPARATION ON THE TRAIL:

1. Add wonton mix and contents of soup packet to 3 cups of water in pot and bring to a boil.
2. Continue to boil until wontons are fully rehydrated.

REQUIRED EQUIPMENT ON THE TRAIL:

Cook pot

Ken Spiegel, Farmingville, New York
Committee Member
Troop 80, Suffolk County Council

TIP:
Wontons and wonton soup mix are available in Asian food markets.

Servings: 2–3
Total Weight: About 4 ounces
Weight per Serving: About 2 ounces
Preparation Time on the Trail: ¼ hour
Challenge Level: Easy

Sawtooth Shrimp Étouffée

3 cups water, added at home

1 large onion, finely chopped

1 bell pepper, finely chopped

2 stalks celery, finely chopped

3 bay leaves

1 teaspoon chili powder

1 standard cube instant beef bouillon

1 teaspoon salt

1 cup long grain rice

1 pound raw peeled and detailed shrimp, chopped into small pieces

1½ cups water per serving, added on the trail

REQUIRED EQUIPMENT ON THE TRAIL:
Cook pot

Lori Neumann, Darlington, Wisconsin
Committee Member
Troop 125, Blackhawk Area Council

"When I first started backpacking, I went alone. I took minimal equipment so as not to carry too much weight, and usually ate M&Ms, Pringles, and cheese. When I met my future husband, I was blown away by all the creative backpack cooking he and his friends did. His friends weren't sure they wanted a girl-type person along on their backpack trips, so I wanted them to think I was too useful to not take along. This was the first main dish I made for them, and with that, they decided I was worth keeping. Since then, I've modified the recipe for use in the camp as well. The title was inspired by the Sawtooth Mountains in Idaho, where my husband and I did much of our backpacking."

PREPARATION AT HOME:

1. Bring 3 cups water to a boil in a cook pot.
2. Add onion, bell pepper, celery, bay leaves, chili powder, bouillon cube, salt, and rice. Stir, cover, and reduce heat to a simmer.
3. After 20 minutes, once the rice is soft, add shrimp and stir.
4. Continue to cook over low heat, about 3 to 5 minutes or until the shrimp turns a light pink. Do not overcook the shrimp or else it will turn rubbery.
5. Remove bay leaves and place about 1½ cups rice mix on each of 4 lined dehydrator trays. Spread each layer as thinly and evenly as possible.
6. Once rice is fully dry, crumble pieces, and place contents from two trays into two 1-quart-size ziplock bags.

PREPARATION ON THE TRAIL:

1. To prepare 1 serving, add the contents of 1 bag of shrimp-rice mix to 1½ cups water and bring to a boil.
2. Cover and simmer until the shrimp and rice are soft.

Servings: 2
Total Weight: 9 ounces
Weight per Serving: About 4 ounces
Preparation Time on the Trail: ¼ hour
Challenge Level: Moderate

Tighty-Whiteys Shrimp and Grits

"On Manitou Island, my oldest son, Ben, had decided he was going to earn his hiking merit badge. We mapped it out, counted paces, but wound up about 2 miles short of his 10 miles. So back at camp, he stripped down to his underwear and took off down the beach. When I paced it off later, I found he'd gone about 3 miles out and 3 miles back, for a total of 14 for the day. I told him he might be the only Scout ever who earned a hiking merit badge while walking in bare feet in his underwear."

¼ cup instant grits

¼ cup dried shrimp

1 tablespoon McCormick Perfect Pinch Roasted Garlic & Bell Pepper seasoning

1 tablespoon dried minced onion

1 tablespoon Nestle Nido whole milk powder

2 tablespoons cheese powder

1¼ cups water, added on the trail

PREPARATION AT HOME:

1. Combine all dry ingredients in a quart-size ziplock bag.

PREPARATION ON THE TRAIL:

1. Pour 1¼ cups water in a pot and add grit mix.
2. Allow pot to rest for a few minutes as the shrimp begins to rehydrate.
3. Bring pot to a boil and cook for 5 to 7 minutes or until the grits soften

REQUIRED EQUIPMENT ON THE TRAIL:

Cook pot

Marc Robinson, Canton, Michigan
Eagle Scout and Assistant Scoutmaster
Troop 854, Great Lakes Council

Option: Shrimp can be purchased already dried, or you can easily dehydrate it yourself. To dry your own, start with frozen, precooked, medium-size shrimp. Thaw, pinch off the tails, and rinse. Slice each shrimp crosswise into 4 or 5 pieces, arrange pieces in a single layer on a dehydrator tray, and dry at about 155°F until firm. There should be no moisture remaining when a piece is cut in half. Refrigerate or freeze until ready to use.

TIP:
Dried powdered cheeses are available from online sources. See Appendix B.

Servings: 1
Total Weight: 3 ounces
Preparation Time on the Trail: ¼ hour
Challenge Level: Easy

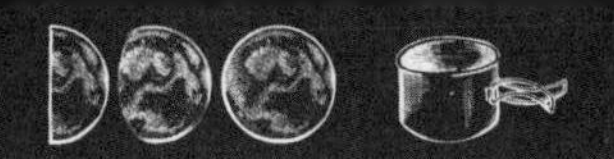

Corn Chowder

- ¾ cup freeze-dried corn
- ½ cup dried potato flakes
- ½ cup Nestle Nido whole milk powder
- ¼ teaspoon ground white pepper
- ¼ teaspoon dried dill weed
- 1 tablespoon dried chives
- 1 tablespoon Butter Buds
- 1 tablespoon dried minced onion
- 1 standard cube instant chicken bouillon
- 2 cups water, added on the trail

PREPARATION AT HOME:

1. Add all dry ingredients to a quart-size ziplock bag.

PREPARATION ON THE TRAIL:

1. Pour dry ingredients into a pot with 2 cups water.
2. Bring to a boil, reduce heat, then simmer until the corn fully rehydrates.

REQUIRED EQUIPMENT ON THE TRAIL:

Cook pot

Tim Conners, Statesboro, Georgia
Assistant Scoutmaster
Troop 340, Coastal Empire Council

Christine Conners, Statesboro, Georgia
Committee Member and Merit Badge Counselor
Troop 340, Coastal Empire Council

Servings: 2
Total Weight: 6 ounces
Weight per Serving: 3 ounces
Preparation Time on the Trail: ¼ hour
Challenge Level: Easy

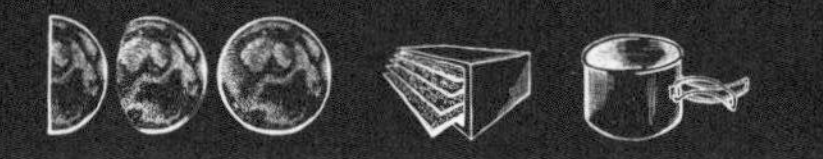

Cimarron Pasta and Beef

"This recipe is named for Cimarron, New Mexico, a town a few miles from Philmont Scout Ranch. I was a Ranger and backcountry camp director at Philmont from 1979 to 1983. I created this recipe for a backpacking trip my troop took along the Ozark Trail in Southern Missouri while we were preparing for our Philmont trek in the summer of 2010."

1½ cups dried lean ground beef (1 pound before drying)

⅔ cup (about 1½ ounces) freeze-dried corn

3 tablespoons Nestle Nido whole milk powder

1 (5.6-ounce) package Hamburger Helper Classic Beef Pasta

4 cups water, added on the trail

Options: This recipe is easily varied by choosing another flavor of Hamburger Helper or by using a different freeze-dried vegetable.

PREPARATION AT HOME:

1. Combine dried ground beef, corn, and milk powder in a quart-size ziplock bag.
2. Remove Hamburger Helper packages from box, but retain in their original bags. Carry separately.

PREPARATION ON THE TRAIL:

1. In a cook pot, add 4 cups of water and the dehydrated ground beef. Bring to a boil.
2. Add contents of Hamburger Helper noodle and sauce mix packages to the hot water.
3. Stir until blended then reduce heat to simmer until noodles are cooked, about 10 minutes. Stir occasionally to reduce sticking.
4. Remove pot from heat. Cover and let rest for about 5 minutes to allow sauce to thicken. Stir and serve.

REQUIRED EQUIPMENT ON THE TRAIL:

Cook pot

Emery Corley, Saint Louis, Missouri
Assistant Scoutmaster
Troop 809, Greater Saint Louis Area Council

Servings: 4
Total Weight: 12 ounces
Weight per Serving: About 3 ounces
Preparation Time on the Trail: ½ hour
Challenge Level: Easy

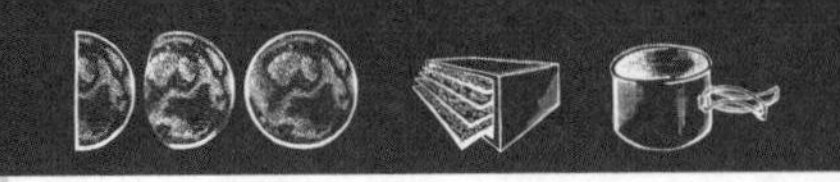

Smokey Mountain Potatoes

"When our Venture Patrol goes backpacking, we cook with a BakePacker, a device that uses boiling water in a standard cook pot to bake foods. It's a method of cooking that virtually eliminates cleanup. This recipe was invented on a Smokey Mountain backpacking adventure several years ago."

1 (5-ounce) box au gratin potatoes, such as Betty Crocker

1½ cups dried lean ground beef (1 pound before drying)

1½ ounces dried broccoli

2 tablespoons Butter Buds or Molly McButter

¼ cup Nestle Nido whole milk powder

3½ cups water, added on the trail, plus additional for BakePacker

Option: If dehydrating your own broccoli, 1 pound fresh broccoli produces about 1–2 ounces dried.

PREPARATION AT HOME:

1. Repackage potatoes in a quart-size ziplock bag, setting aside the cheese mix packet for Step 3.
2. Combine dried beef and broccoli in a quart-size ziplock bag.
3. To a third quart-size ziplock bag, add Butter Buds, milk powder, and cheese mix from the box of potatoes.
4. Place individual quart-size bags into a gallon-size ziplock bag along with an oven bag and a copy of these directions.

PREPARATION ON THE TRAIL:

1. Place BakePacker grid in pot then fill pot with water to the top of the grid.
2. Pour contents from each of the three ziplock bags into the oven bag and add 3½ cups of water. Mix thoroughly but carefully so as to not puncture the bag.
3. Lay oven bag evenly over grid. Fold top of bag down like you would roll a sleeping bag. Do not seal with a twist tie.
4. Cover pot, place pot on stove, and heat to boiling.
5. Continue at a boil for 25 minutes then check to see if potatoes, broccoli, and meat are fully soft. If not, continue cooking. If water level becomes low, add more water.

REQUIRED EQUIPMENT ON THE TRAIL:

4-quart cook pot with lid
Standard-size (7⅜-inch) BakePacker
1 large-size (not "turkey-size") oven bag

TIPS:

- Be sure the BakePacker grid fits within your pot before leaving for the trail.
- Carry an extra oven bag in the event the first one punctures.
- Soaking the beef-broccoli mix in a little water while setting up camp will improve its texture during baking. Drain excess water from bag before using.
- Be sure the water doesn't fully evaporate during cooking or else the oven bag will melt.
- See recipe for Great Lakes Ground Beef for instructions on dehydrating ground meats.

Servings: 4
Total Weight: 12 ounces
Weight per Serving: 3 ounces
Preparation Time on the Trail: ¾ hour
Challenge Level: Moderate

Linda Nosalik, Upper Marlboro, Maryland
Assistant Scoutmaster and Venture Patrol Adviser
Troop 1575, National Capital Area Council

Super Sushi Rolls

2 sheets nori seaweed

2 tablespoons tamanoi sushinoko (powdered sushi seasoning)

1 tablespoon furikake or gomasio (sesame seeds and seasoning with nori flakes)

1 (3½-ounce) pouch boil-in-bag jasmine rice

1 (2½-ounce) pouch cooked tuna or salmon

Optional: dried tofu, dried mushrooms, soy sauce packet, salt

1 quart water, added on the trail

REQUIRED EQUIPMENT ON THE TRAIL:
Cook pot

PREPARATION AT HOME:

1. Seal seaweed sheets flat in a gallon-size ziplock bag.
2. In a small ziplock bag or container, combine sushi seasoning and furikake or gomasio seasoning.
3. Pack rice, fish pouch, and any optional items separately.

PREPARATION ON THE TRAIL:

1. Leaving it in its cooking pouch, boil rice in a quart of water for about 10 minutes along with optional dried tofu or dried mushrooms.
2. Drain water from pot, open rice pouch, and pour rice into pot. Cool the rice by spreading it out in the pot and fanning it with your hand or pot lid.
3. When rice is no longer hot, sprinkle with powdered seasoning. Mix well, being careful not to mash the rice.
4. Lay 1 square sheet of nori on top of the gallon-size bag on a flat surface, dull side of the nori sheet facing up.
5. Place half the rice mixture onto the nori and spread to cover most of the surface.
6. Dividing the tuna or salmon in half, flake some of the fish onto the rice mixture along a line near an edge of the nori.
7. Being sure to reserve plenty for the sushi roll that remains to be prepared, also spread some of the fish and seasoning over the rice.
8. Using the plastic bag as a firm base, roll the bag along with the sushi into a cylinder, being sure not to wrap the plastic into the sushi roll.
9. Wet the final edge of the nori then gently apply pressure through the plastic bag to seal the whole roll.
10. The roll can be cut into slices using a very sharp, thin knife. Or just eat it like a wrap sandwich. Garnish with optional salt or soy sauce.
11. Repeat steps 4 though 10 to produce the second sushi roll.

TIPS: If the nori sheets crumble, place ingredients in a pot or bowl. This is called "chirashi," which means "scattered sushi."

Servings: 2–3
Total Weight: 7 ounces
Weight per Serving: About 3 ounces
Preparation Time on the Trail: ¾ hour
Challenge Level: Difficult

Curt "The Titanium Chef" White, Forks, Washington
Committee Member
Troop 1467, Chief Seattle Council

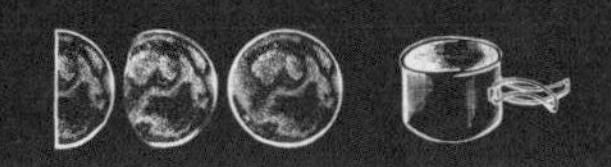

Mediterranean Ramen

2 (3-ounce) packages ramen noodles (any flavor)

1 (1.2-ounce) packet Knorr Creamy Pesto sauce mix

1 tablespoon grated Parmesan cheese

¼ cup pine nuts

3 tablespoons olive oil

Optional: dried capers to taste

2 cups water, added on the trail

"Plain instant ramen gets boring quickly, but the noodle itself is quite versatile. I love Mediterranean flavors, and this idea came to me when I spotted pesto and dried sauce mixes at the store."

PREPARATION AT HOME:

1. Retain ramen noodles and pesto sauce in their original packaging.
2. Package cheese and pine nuts together in a small ziplock bag.
3. Carry olive oil and optional capers separately.

PREPARATION ON THE TRAIL:

1. Bring 2 cups water to a boil in a pot and add ramen noodles and optional capers to rehydrate. Set aside ramen seasoning packets. They aren't used for this recipe.
2. Meanwhile, add oil to pesto envelope and stir to make a thin paste.
3. Once the noodles and optional capers have rehydrated, pour pesto mix on top of the noodles and stir to coat.
4. Sprinkle cheese and pine nuts over noodles and serve.

REQUIRED EQUIPMENT ON THE TRAIL:

Cook pot

Curt "The Titanium Chef" White, Forks, Washington
Committee Member
Troop 1467, Chief Seattle Council

Servings: 2
Total Weight: 11 ounces
Weight per Serving: About 5 ounces
Preparation Time on the Trail: ¼ hour
Challenge Level: Easy

Rocket Chili

"We all know that fiber is good for the body. Well, the incredible fibrousity in each serving of this delicious recipe is especially so, probably capable of generating enough methane to fuel NASA's latest launch vehicle. When dinner is over, the fun is just beginning with Rocket Chili."

1 (15-ounce) can black beans

1 (15-ounce) can kidney beans

1 (14½-ounce) can stewed tomatoes

1 (10¾-ounce) can tomato soup

1 medium onion, diced

1 green pepper, diced

1 clove garlic, minced

1 cup frozen white corn

¼ teaspoon cayenne powder

¼ cup maple syrup

1½ cups water per serving, added on the trail

Optional: dried lean ground beef, added on the trail

PREPARATION AT HOME:

1. Drain and rinse beans then pour into a pot.
2. Drain the tomatoes then chop and add to the beans in the pot.
3. Combine the remainder of the ingredients, except for water, in the pot and simmer over low heat until the diced onions are thoroughly cooked.
4. Pour about 2 cups chili mixture onto each of 3 parchment or plastic-lined dehydrator trays. Spread thinly and evenly. Each tray will produce 1 serving.
5. Thoroughly dry the chili in the dehydrator.
6. Crumble each sheet of dried chili mix into its own quart-size ziplock bag.
7. Package optional dried ground beef separately.

PREPARATION ON THE TRAIL:

1. To prepare 1 serving, bring 1½ cups water to a boil.
2. Tear the chili leather from one ziplock bag into small pieces and add to the boiling water.
3. Add optional ground beef at this time. If ground beef is used, a little extra water may need to be added depending on the quantity of meat to be rehydrated.
4. Reduce heat and stir occasionally until fully rehydrated.

TIP:
See recipe for Great Lakes Ground Beef for instructions on dehydrating ground meats.

REQUIRED EQUIPMENT ON THE TRAIL:

Cook pot

Tim Conners, Statesboro, Georgia
Assistant Scoutmaster
Troop 340, Coastal Empire Council

Christine Conners, Statesboro, Georgia
Committee Member and Merit Badge Counselor
Troop 340, Coastal Empire Council

Servings: 3
Total Weight: 12 ounces
Weight per Serving: 4 ounces
Preparation Time on the Trail: ¼ hour
Challenge Level: Easy

ABC Chili

1 pound lean ground beef

1 medium onion, diced

1 (14½-ounce) can kidney beans, drained

1 (15-ounce) can tomato sauce

1 (14½-ounce) can diced tomatoes

1 (1¼-ounce) packet McCormick chili seasoning mix

2 tablespoons granulated sugar

2 cups water, added at home

1 (12-ounce) bag DaVinci alphabet pasta

1¼ cups water per serving, added on the trail

PREPARATION AT HOME:

1. Brown ground beef in a pan along with the onion until beef is fully cooked.
2. Drain any liquid and transfer beef and onions to a pot.
3. Add beans, tomato sauce, diced tomatoes with juice, seasoning mix, sugar, and 2 cups water.
4. Bring to a boil then reduce heat and add alphabet pasta.
5. Simmer pasta until tender, about 5 to 10 minutes.
6. Place about 1½ cups chili onto each of 5 dehydrator trays, spreading the mixture thinly on each tray.
7. Once dry, place content from each tray into its own quart-size ziplock bag.
8. Label each of the 5 bags with the name of the recipe and the water required to rehydrate it on the trail.

PREPARATION ON THE TRAIL:

1. For 1 serving, tear chili leather from 1 ziplock bag into small pieces and add to a pot along with 1¼ cups of water. Bring to a boil.
2. Reduce heat and simmer for about 10 minutes or until fully rehydrated.

REQUIRED EQUIPMENT ON THE TRAIL:

Cook pot

Ken Spiegel, Farmingville, New York
Committee Member
Troop 80, Suffolk County Council

Servings: 5
Total Weight: 1 pound 6 ounces
Weight per Serving: About 5 ounces
Preparation Time on the Trail: ¼ hour
Challenge Level: Easy

Venison Cinnamon Sweet Beans

1 pound ground venison or lean ground beef

1 large onion, chopped fine

1 large bell pepper, chopped fine

2 (28-ounce) cans Bush's vegetarian baked beans

1 teaspoon ground cinnamon

1¼ cups water per serving, added on the trail

PREPARATION AT HOME:

1. In a pan or Dutch oven, sauté venison along with onion and bell pepper until venison is no longer pink. Drain excess liquid.
2. Add baked beans and cinnamon, stir, then simmer for about 5 minutes.
3. Place about 1½ cups venison-bean mixture onto each of 6 lined dehydrator trays. Dry until brittle.
4. Divide contents from the dryer trays among 6 quart-size ziplock bags.

PREPARATION ON THE TRAIL:

1. For each serving of beans, combine with 1¼ cups water in a pot.
2. Bring to a boil, cover, then simmer until beans and meat are fully rehydrated.

REQUIRED EQUIPMENT ON THE TRAIL:

Cook pot

Tim Conners, Statesboro, Georgia
Assistant Scoutmaster
Troop 340, Coastal Empire Council

Christine Conners, Statesboro, Georgia
Committee Member and Merit Badge Counselor
Troop 340, Coastal Empire Council

Servings: 6
Total Weight: 1 pound 11 ounces
Weight per Serving: About 5 ounces
Preparation Time on the Trail: ¼ hour
Challenge Level: Easy

Appalachian Chicken and Rice

1 cup instant brown rice

¼ cup dried mushrooms

2 tablespoons onion flakes

1 tablespoon McCormick Perfect Pinch Roasted Garlic & Bell Pepper seasoning

1 (7-ounce) pouch cooked chicken

1 (0.6-ounce) envelope Cream of Chicken flavor Lipton Cup-a-Soup

2½ cups water, added on the trail

Option: On shorter trips, or if used within 1 day of leaving the trailhead, a 1-ounce mini brick of cream cheese can be blended into the rice during the last few minutes of simmering to add a creamy texture.

PREPARATION AT HOME:

1. Combine rice, dried mushrooms, onion flakes, and seasoning in a quart-size ziplock bag.
2. Carry chicken pouch and soup mix envelope separately.

PREPARATION ON THE TRAIL:

1. In a pot with 2½ cups of water, add contents of rice bag and soup mix.
2. Heat to boiling, stir, then reduce heat and simmer for about 5 minutes.
3. Stir in the chicken and continue to simmer for an additional 3 to 5 minutes or until the rice becomes soft.

REQUIRED EQUIPMENT ON THE TRAIL:
Cook pot

Joseph E. Brown, Huntsville, Alabama
District Commissioner
Korea District, Far East Council

Servings: 2–3
Total Weight: 13 ounces
Weight per Serving: About 6 ounces
Preparation Time on the Trail: ¼ hour
Challenge Level: Easy

Backpacker's Tortellini

2 (5-ounce) packets Boboli pizza sauce

1 (12-ounce) package Barilla dry cheese tortellini

1 quart water, added on the trail

PREPARATION AT HOME:

1. Carry sauce and tortellini separately.

PREPARATION ON THE TRAIL:

1. Add sauce to 4 cups water in a pot and bring to a boil.
2. Add tortellini and continue boiling for about 10 minutes, or until the pasta softens.

REQUIRED EQUIPMENT ON THE TRAIL:

Cook pot

Tim Conners, Statesboro, Georgia
Assistant Scoutmaster
Troop 340, Coastal Empire Council

Christine Conners, Statesboro, Georgia
Committee Member and Merit Badge Counselor
Troop 340, Coastal Empire Council

Troop 486 at Philmont Scout Ranch. *MAX COLES*

Servings: 3–4
Total Weight: 1 pound 6 ounces
Weight per Serving: About 6 ounces
Preparation Time on the Trail: ¼ hour
Challenge Level: Easy

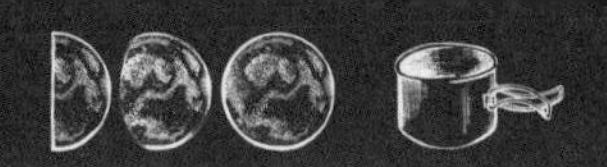

Tetons Tuna Fish Casserole

½ cup Just Veggies brand freeze-dried vegetable mix

3 tablespoons Nestle Nido whole powdered milk

1 (7¼-ounce) package Kraft Macaroni and Cheese

1 (2½-ounce) foil pouch cooked tuna in water

3 cups water, added on the trail

Option: In place of the freeze-dried vegetable mix, a frozen vegetable mix from the grocer can be thawed and dried in a home food dehydrator for this recipe.

PREPARATION AT HOME:

1. Package dried vegetables and milk powder together in a quart-size ziplock bag.
2. Repackage macaroni noodles into a second quart-size bag.
3. Carry powdered macaroni cheese mix and tuna in their original packaging.

PREPARATION ON THE TRAIL:

1. Pour 3 cups water in a pot and add dried vegetable mix. Allow to rest for about 5 minutes.
2. Bring water to a boil. Add noodles, stir, and cook until macaroni becomes soft.
3. Reduce heat. Stir in cheese powder and tuna then serve.

REQUIRED EQUIPMENT ON THE TRAIL:

Cook pot

Marc Robinson, Canton, Michigan
Eagle Scout and Assistant Scoutmaster
Troop 854, Great Lakes Council

Servings: 2
Total Weight: 12 ounces
Weight per Serving: 6 ounces
Preparation Time on the Trail: ½ hour
Challenge Level: Easy

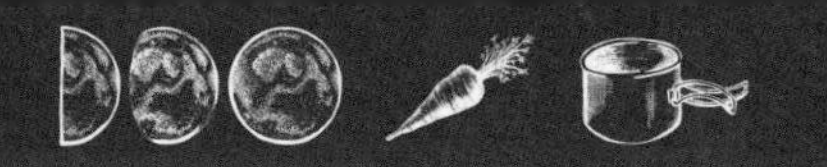

Vent-the-Tent Burritos

"If you prepare this for dinner, make sure the vents on your tent are open when retiring for the evening. If you make it for lunch, it's just the thing to provide some 'wind power' to climb those afternoon inclines."

1 (5.6-ounce) package Knorr Fiesta Sides Spanish rice

1 (7-ounce) package Fantastic Foods refried beans

½ cup grated Parmesan cheese

4 burrito-size tortillas

4 cups water, added on the trail

PREPARATION AT HOME:

1. In a gallon-size heavy-duty ziplock bag, combine rice, beans, and cheese.
2. Carry tortillas separately.

PREPARATION ON THE TRAIL:

1. Bring 4 cups water to a boil and remove from heat.
2. Set ziplock bag containing rice-bean mixture in a cook pot to stabilize it.
3. Once boiling subsides, pour hot water into rice-bean bag.
4. Carefully knead the bag to remove clumps and allow bag to rest until beans and rice are fully rehydrated.
5. Cut a corner from the bottom of the bag and squirt rice-bean mix into each of the 4 tortillas.
6. Roll each tortilla like a burrito and serve.

REQUIRED EQUIPMENT ON THE TRAIL:

Cook pot

Options: Add taco sauce (from condiment packs), rehydrated ground beef, salsa, onions, bell peppers, or tomatoes to make the burritos truly authentic.

Rob Petz, Rockton, Illinois
Scoutmaster
Troop 619, Glacier's Edge Council

Servings: 4
Total Weight: 1 pound 9 ounces
Weight per Serving: About 6 ounces
Preparation Time on the Trail: ½ hour
Challenge Level: Easy

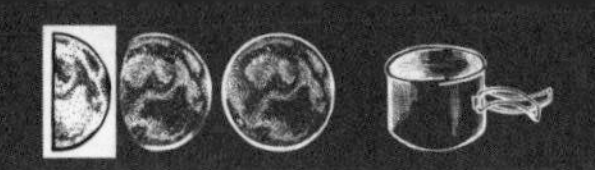

Frat Boy's Goulash

2 (3-ounce) packages chicken or creamy chicken ramen noodles

1 (7-ounce) pouch cooked cubed chicken

Optional: Spam, Parmesan cheese, dried onion, dried seaweed, dried mushrooms, dried cuttlefish, dried tofu, or crushed red pepper

2 cups water, added on the trail

Option: To create a thick pasta recipe instead of soup, cut the water added on the trail to 1 cup.

"This recipe is quick, easy, hot, cheap, filling, great tasting, weighs less than 1 pound, and uses only one pot. As any college kid will tell you, there really is no end to the various recipes that can be made using ramen noodles. Asian stores, in particular, provide a nice variety of dried ingredients that go great with ramen."

PREPARATION AT HOME:

1. Carry ramen, chicken, and any optional ingredients separately in their original packaging.

PREPARATION ON THE TRAIL:

1. Bring 2 cups water to a boil, add ramen, and cook until noodles soften, a matter of seconds.
2. Add contents of the flavor packets along with the chicken and any optional ingredients.
3. Stir until well-mixed and heated all the way through.

REQUIRED EQUIPMENT ON THE TRAIL:

Cook pot

Mark Corbelli, Richmond, Virginia
Assistant Scoutmaster
Troop 893, Heart of Virginia Council

Servings: 2
Total Weight: 13 ounces
Weight per Serving: About 7 ounces
Preparation Time on the Trail: ¼ hour
Challenge Level: Easy

Sweet & Sour Rice

1½ cups instant white rice

½ cup Just Carrots brand freeze-dried carrots

½ cup chopped candied pineapple tidbits

¼ cup bell pepper flakes

2 tablespoons dried minced onion

¼ cup sun-dried tomato, chopped

2 tablespoons brown sugar

1 (0.75-ounce) packet Sun Bird or Sun Luck brand sweet and sour sauce mix

3 cups water, added on the trail

PREPARATION AT HOME:

1. Thoroughly mix all dry ingredients and store in a quart-size ziplock bag.

PREPARATION ON THE TRAIL:

1. Bring 3 cups water and dry mixture to a boil.
2. Stir occasionally for 5 minutes before serving.

REQUIRED EQUIPMENT ON THE TRAIL:

Cook pot

Ken Harbison, Rochester, New York
Former Boy Scout and Master Tester for *The Scout's Outdoor Cookbook*
Washington Trail Council

Servings: 2
Total Weight: 14 ounces
Weight per Serving: 7 ounces
Preparation Time on the Trail: ¼ hour
Challenge Level: Easy

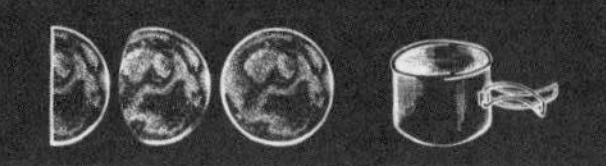

Klondike Thai Peanut Shrimp

½ cup Nestle Nido whole powdered milk

½ cup shredded coconut

1 (3½-ounce) envelope A Taste of Thai peanut sauce mix

2 (3-ounce) packages ramen noodles (discard flavoring packages)

1 (4-ounce) can Chicken of the Sea shrimp

2 tablespoons vegetable oil

2 tablespoons chopped peanuts

2 cups water, added on the trail

"I first made this recipe at our council's Klondike Derby snow camping event. You would think that, as a Scout leader 'always prepared,' I would have tested it at home first. Well, no, I didn't. But it turned out great anyway and has been one of my backpacking staples ever since."

PREPARATION AT HOME:

1. In a blender, pulverize milk powder and shredded coconut together.
2. Place coconut-milk powder in a small ziplock bag.
3. Carry Thai sauce mix, ramen noodles, shrimp, oil, and peanuts separately.

PREPARATION ON THE TRAIL:

1. Add coconut-milk powder, Thai sauce mix, and oil to 2 cups water. Stir then bring to a boil.
2. Add ramen noodles and shrimp, along with liquid from can, to the boiling water.
3. Continue to cook for about 3 minutes or until noodles become soft.
4. Garnish with chopped peanuts and serve.

REQUIRED EQUIPMENT ON THE TRAIL:

Cook pot
Can opener

Gordon Abraham, Los Altos, California
Assistant Scoutmaster
Troop 37, Pacific Skyline Council

Servings: 2–3
Total Weight: 1 pound
Weight per Serving: About 7 ounces
Preparation Time on the Trail: ¼ hour
Challenge Level: Moderate

Ramen Italia

"Because ramen is designed to be rapidly rehydrated, it can be used to make a quick spaghetti dish that saves backpackers' time, fuel, and water."

1 (3-ounce) packet instant ramen noodles

1 (5-ounce) packet Boboli pizza sauce

Optional seasonings: garlic powder; dried basil; dried oregano; dried onion powder; grated Parmesan cheese; red pepper flakes; dried kalamata olives, green olives, or capers

1½ cups water, added on the trail

PREPARATION AT HOME:

1. Pack ramen noodles and pizza sauce for the trail in their original packaging.
2. Combine any optional seasonings in a ziplock bag or seasoning container.

PREPARATION ON THE TRAIL:

1. In a pot, bring water to a boil and add ramen noodles. Discard the seasoning packet; it isn't used with this recipe.
2. Return water to a boil then continue to cook until noodles are tender. This won't take long.
3. Remove pot from heat and drain any remaining water.
4. Add Boboli sauce and any optional ingredients then stir well. Buon appetito.

REQUIRED EQUIPMENT ON THE TRAIL:
Cook pot

Curt "The Titanium Chef" White, Forks, Washington
Committee Member
Troop 1467, Chief Seattle Council

Servings: 1
Total Weight: 8 ounces
Preparation Time on Trail: 5 minutes
Challenge Level: Easy

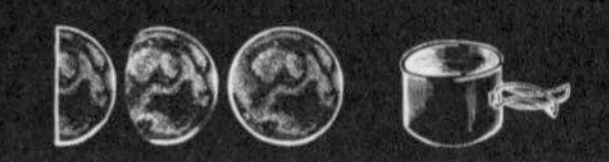

Jerky Spiced Rice

3 ounces beef jerky (your favorite)

½ cup Minute Rice

5 single-serving packets mild taco sauce

5 single-serving packets ketchup

1 cup water, added on the trail

"My troop likes this recipe because it is easy and fairly lightweight to carry. I developed it just to show the boys that there are good alternatives to expensive, and sometimes tasteless, freeze-dried meals."

PREPARATION AT HOME:

1. Chop beef jerky into ½-inch-thick pieces and place in a quart-size ziplock bag.
2. Add rice to the jerky bag.
3. Carry taco sauce and ketchup packets separately.

PREPARATION ON THE TRAIL:

1. Pour 1 cup water in a pot. Add taco sauce and ketchup and bring to a boil.
2. Add rice-jerky mix and stir.
3. Serve once rice and jerky become tender.

REQUIRED EQUIPMENT ON THE TRAIL:

Cook pot

Dale Price, Pleasant Garden, North Carolina
Committee Chair
Troop 342, Old North State Council

TIP:
Don't throw away those extra taco sauce and ketchup packets from the fast-food restaurant; use them for recipes like this. Condiment packets are also available in bulk from online retailers; see Appendix B.

Servings: 1
Total Weight: 8 ounces
Preparation Time on the Trail: ¼ hour
Challenge Level: Easy

Cluckin' Mac n' Cheese

"Everyone loves mac n' cheese. But we needed something more substantial because the Scouts were striving for 10 miles per day. Everyone loved this."

1 (12-ounce) box Velveeta Shells and Cheese

1 (7-ounce) foil pouch cooked chicken

2½ cups water, added on the trail

PREPARATION AT HOME:

1. Remove noodles from the package and carry in a quart-size ziplock bag.
2. Carry cheese and chicken separately in their original packages.

PREPARATION ON THE TRAIL:

1. Bring 2½ cups water to a boil in a pot.
2. Add noodles and allow to cook until soft.
3. Remove from heat, add cheese and chicken, stir, and serve.

REQUIRED EQUIPMENT ON THE TRAIL:

Cook pot

Collin McGrath, Weston, Florida
Eagle Scout and Troop Guide
Troop 383, South Florida Council

Servings: 2–3
Total Weight: 1¼ pounds
Weight per Serving: About 8 ounces
Preparation Time on the Trail: ¼ hour
Challenge Level: Easy

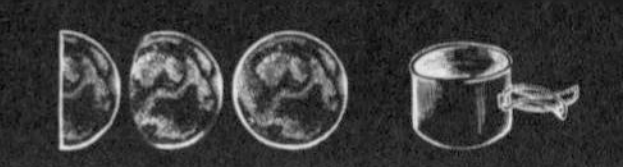

Tall Pines Chicken and Dumplings

"More work than a freeze-dried meal in a pouch, but well worth the effort."

1 standard cube instant chicken bouillon

½ cup Just Veggies brand freeze-dried vegetable mix

½ teaspoon dried parsley

½ teaspoon crushed dried rosemary

½ teaspoon dried thyme

1 teaspoon dried minced onion

1 (8-ounce) package Jiffy buttermilk biscuit mix

1 (7-ounce) pouch cooked chicken

2 cups water, added on the trail

Option: In place of the freeze-dried vegetable mix, a frozen vegetable mix from the grocer can be thawed and dried in a home food dehydrator for this recipe.

PREPARATION AT HOME:

1. In a quart-size ziplock bag, combine bouillon cube, dried vegetable mix, parsley, rosemary, thyme, and onion.
2. Pour biscuit mix in a quart-size heavy-duty ziplock bag.
3. Retain chicken in its original foil pouch.

PREPARATION ON THE TRAIL:

1. Combine dried vegetables and spices with chicken and 1½ cups water in a pot. Bring to a boil.
2. Prepare biscuit dough by adding ½ cup water to the biscuit mix bag and kneading the bag well.
3. Cut a corner from the dough bag and squeeze blobs of dumpling dough into the stew. Cover and simmer.
4. Steam until biscuits are fully cooked then serve.

REQUIRED EQUIPMENT ON THE TRAIL:

Cook pot

Judy Gratsch, Grand Blanc, Michigan
Assistant Scoutmaster
Troop 176, Tall Pine Council

Servings: 2–3
Total Weight: 1 pound 2 ounces
Weight per Serving: About 8 ounces
Preparation Time on the Trail: ½ hour
Challenge Level: Moderate

Thanksgiving on the Trail

1 (4-ounce) package Idahoan Loaded Baked flavored mashed potatoes

¼ cup Nestle Nido whole milk powder

½ cup dried herbed stuffing mix (your choice)

¾ cup Craisins

1 (10-ounce) can chicken breast

1 teaspoon olive oil

2 cups water, added on the trail

PREPARATION AT HOME:

1. Combine potato flakes, powdered milk, stuffing mix, and Craisins in a quart-size ziplock bag.
2. Carry can of chicken and olive oil separately.

PREPARATION ON THE TRAIL:

1. Heat 2 cups water to a boil and add olive oil. Remove from heat.
2. Add the dry ingredients to the pot and stir well.
3. Add chicken with juice, stir, and serve while hot.

REQUIRED EQUIPMENT ON THE TRAIL:

Cook pot
Can opener

Chad Kinsey, Mount Airy, Georgia
Den Leader
Pack 24, Northeast Georgia Council

Servings: 2–3
Total Weight: 1½ pounds
Weight per Serving: About 10 ounces
Preparation Time on the Trail: ¼ hour
Challenge Level: Easy

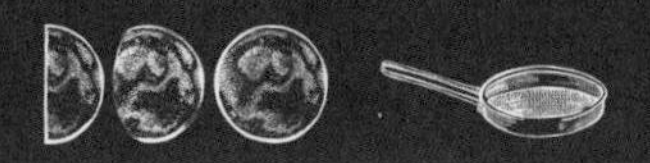

Slippery Hook's Fish Fry

1 cup unbleached white wheat flour

½ cup cornmeal

1 tablespoon Old Bay seasoning

1 cup safflower or sunflower oil

2 pounds filleted smallmouth bass or northern pike, caught on the trail

Caution: When frying in hot oil over an open fire, always have a lid handy so that if the oil catches fire, the flames can be suffocated with the lid. Never pour water on an oil fire nor attempt to remove the flaming pan from the stove.

TIP:
The oil is hot enough to begin frying once a small piece of fish tossed into the pan begins to immediately bubble. The temperature is too hot if the oil begins to smoke. Immediately lower the flame if this occurs.

Servings: 6–7
Total Weight: 1 pound 1 ounce
Weight per Serving: About 3 ounces
Preparation Time on Trail: ¼ hour (not including cleaning the fish)
Challenge Level: Easy (unless the fish aren't biting!)

"My boys and I were on a weeklong trip to the Boundary Waters Canoe Area Wilderness. Despite our many attempts, we hadn't caught any fish. After getting our campsite in order several days into the trip, my son Devin begged to try again at upper Horseshoe Falls. He cast into the grassy area, and BOOM, a smallmouth bass grabbed his lure. It immediately jumped out of the water and looked to be over 4 pounds. The bass put up a big fight. But fishing in a canoe is hard. If your fishing partner moves around a lot while you're bringing one in, you can lose your balance . . . and your fish. Needless to say, that's exactly what happened. Ouch. Was Devin mad at me!"

PREPARATION AT HOME:

1. Mix all dry ingredients together in a gallon-size heavy-duty ziplock bag.
2. Carry oil separately.

PREPARATION ON THE TRAIL:

1. First and foremost: Catch fish along the trail.
2. Place cleaned fish fillets into flour mix in the ziplock bag and shake to thoroughly coat.
3. Heat oil in a deep frying pan.
4. Using spatula or tongs, carefully place several pieces of coated fish at a time into hot oil, frying for 3 minutes per side before serving.
5. Promptly remove the pan from the flame once finished cooking.

REQUIRED EQUIPMENT ON THE TRAIL:

Deep skillet and lid
Metal spatula or tongs

John Bostick, Cincinnati, Ohio
Eagle Scout and Former Assistant Scoutmaster
Troop 375, Buffalo Trace Council

Voyager Pan Puppies

"My parents served us hush puppies as kids, and Dad had several variations that he used when he was a canoe guide at the Charles Sommers Canoe Base in Ely, Minnesota. This is one of his versions I adapted for backpacking."

2 cups instant cornmeal
1 teaspoon salt
1 teaspoon baking powder
¼ cup whole egg powder
½ cup chopped figs
½ teaspoon ground cinnamon
¼ teaspoon ground nutmeg
1 tablespoon brown sugar
¼ cup canola oil
Optional: Jam, honey, or syrup
2 cups water, added on the trail

PREPARATION AT HOME:

1. In a gallon-size heavy-duty ziplock bag, combine cornmeal, salt, baking powder, egg powder, figs, cinnamon, nutmeg, and brown sugar.
2. Carry oil and optional ingredients separately.

PREPARATION ON THE TRAIL:

1. Add 2 cups water to the cornmeal bag and knead until contents become a soft dough.
2. Heat oil in a fry pan until a drop of water dances on the surface. Meanwhile, roll dough into golf ball-size balls then flatten between palms.
3. Fry puppies until golden brown on each side.
4. Serve with optional jam, honey, or syrup.

REQUIRED EQUIPMENT ON THE TRAIL:

Skillet
Spatula

Curt "The Titanium Chef" White, Forks, Washington
Committee Member
Troop 1467, Chief Seattle Council

TIP:
Instant cornmeal can be found in the Hispanic foods section at the grocery store.

Servings: 6
Total Weight: 1 pound 1 ounce
Weight per Serving: About 3 ounces
Preparation Time on the Trail: ½ hour
Challenge Level: Moderate

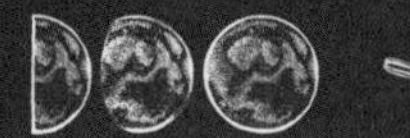

Hot n' Spicy Potato Cakes

2 cups instant potato flakes

¼ cup all-purpose flour

3 tablespoons dried whole egg powder

½ teaspoon salt

¼ teaspoon ground black pepper

1 tablespoon dried parsley flakes

⅛ teaspoon garlic powder

¼ cup grated Parmesan cheese

Optional: 1 teaspoon red pepper flakes

½ cup canola oil

1½ cups water, added on the trail

"I adapted a traditional recipe for potato cakes by using lighter ingredients and dried herbs and spices for backpacking. I enjoy spicy dishes, but it tastes great even without the hot pepper flakes."

PREPARATION AT HOME:

1. In a quart-size heavy-duty ziplock bag, combine potato flakes, flour, egg powder, salt, black pepper, parsley, garlic powder, Parmesan cheese, and, if you can take the heat, red pepper flakes.
2. Carry oil separately.

PREPARATION ON THE TRAIL:

1. Add 1½ cups water to ziplock bag and knead until potatoes become a soft dough.
2. Flatten potato mixture into several patties.
3. Heat oil in frying pan until a drop of water dances on the oil, then fry patties until golden brown, about a minute or two on each side.

REQUIRED EQUIPMENT ON THE TRAIL:

Skillet
Spatula

Curt "The Titanium Chef" White, Forks, Washington
Committee Member
Troop 1467, Chief Seattle Council

Servings: 3
Total Weight: 11 ounces
Weight per Serving: About 4 ounces
Preparation Time on the Trail: ½ hour
Challenge Level: Moderate

Fremont Fish Cakes

PREPARATION AT HOME:

1. In a quart-size heavy-duty ziplock bag, combine potato flakes, Italian seasoning, onion, garlic, egg powder, salt, lemon-pepper, and Butter Buds.
2. Carry salmon pouch and oil separately.

PREPARATION ON THE TRAIL:

1. Add ⅓ cup water to potato bag along with contents of salmon pouch. Knead the bag.
2. Form potato-fish mix into 2 large or 4 small patties.
3. Fry patties in oil until both sides become a light brown.

REQUIRED EQUIPMENT ON THE TRAIL:

Skillet
Spatula

Tim Conners, Statesboro, Georgia
Assistant Scoutmaster
Troop 340, Coastal Empire Council

Christine Conners, Statesboro, Georgia
Committee Member and Merit Badge Counselor
Troop 340, Coastal Empire Council

1 cup instant potato flakes

1 tablespoon Italian seasoning spice blend

1 teaspoon minced onion

1 teaspoon minced garlic

2 tablespoons whole egg powder

¼ teaspoon salt

½ teaspoon lemon and pepper seasoning

1 tablespoon Butter Buds

1 (6-ounce) pouch cooked pink salmon

2 tablespoons vegetable oil

⅓ cup water, added on the trail

Option: Mayo packets and pita bread make this a feast.

Servings: 2
Total Weight: 10 ounces
Weight per Serving: 5 ounces
Preparation Time on the Trail: ¼ hour
Challenge Level: Easy

Bechtel Broccoli and Hollandaise Sauce

2 pounds frozen chopped or cut broccoli, thawed

1 (1¼-ounce) package McCormick Hollandaise Sauce mix

¼ cup (½ standard stick) butter

3 cups water, added on the trail

Caution: Butter can be left unrefrigerated for 1 or 2 days, but after that, it will spoil rapidly.

TIP:
Dehydrated broccoli retains a slightly wilted look when it is reconstituted. Regardless, it still tastes great.

"Named in honor of The Summit Bechtel Reserve, BSA's newest high-adventure base, located in the mountains of West Virginia."

PREPARATION AT HOME:

1. Dry broccoli in dehydrator.
2. Place dried broccoli in a quart-size ziplock bag. Add dry hollandaise sauce mix packet to the bag.
3. Carry butter separately.

PREPARATION ON THE TRAIL:

1. Add dried broccoli, hollandaise mix, and butter to 3 cups water in a pot and bring to a boil.
2. Reduce heat, cover, and simmer until broccoli is soft, about 15 minutes.

REQUIRED EQUIPMENT ON THE TRAIL:
Cook pot

Tim Conners, Statesboro, Georgia
Assistant Scoutmaster
Troop 340, Coastal Empire Council

Christine Conners, Statesboro, Georgia
Committee Member and Merit Badge Counselor
Troop 340, Coastal Empire Council

Servings: 3–4
Total Weight: 7 ounces
Weight per Serving: About 2 ounces
Preparation Time on the Trail: ¼ hour
Challenge Level: Easy

Pikes Peak Potato Soup

½ cup instant potato flakes

½ cup Nestle Nido whole milk powder

¼ cup whole-wheat flour

1 tablespoon dried minced chives

1 teaspoon dried parsley flakes

¾ teaspoon salt

8 ounces cheddar cheese

4 cups water, added on the trail

PREPARATION AT HOME:

1. In a quart-size ziplock bag, combine potato flakes, milk powder, flour, chives, parsley, and salt.
2. Carry cheese separately.

PREPARATION ON THE TRAIL:

1. In a pot, add potato mix to 4 cups water. Bring to a boil.
2. Slice the cheese into small cubes.
3. Once potato soup has thickened, reduce heat, and add cheese cubes to the pot.
4. Stir until cheese has fully melted then serve.

REQUIRED EQUIPMENT ON THE TRAIL:

Cook pot

Tim Conners, Statesboro, Georgia
Assistant Scoutmaster
Troop 340, Coastal Empire Council

Christine Conners, Statesboro, Georgia
Committee Member and Merit Badge Counselor
Troop 340, Coastal Empire Council

Servings: 3–4
Total Weight: 12 ounces
Weight per Serving: About 4 ounces
Preparation Time on the Trail: ¼ hour
Challenge Level: Easy

BSA Beef Stroganoff

¼ cup dried lean ground beef

¼ cup Just Veggies brand freeze-dried vegetable mix

1 teaspoon paprika

1 dash cayenne pepper

1 (3-ounce) package beef-flavored ramen noodles, with seasoning packet

1 (1-ounce) mini-brick Philadelphia cream cheese

1½ cups water, added on the trail

Option: In place of the freeze-dried vegetable mix, a frozen vegetable mix from the grocer can be thawed and dried in a home food dehydrator for this recipe.

Caution: Cream cheese should not be left unrefrigerated for a long period of time because of the risk of spoilage. Do not carry cream cheese on the trail if the weather will be very warm, and use any that you do carry within a day or so after taking it out of the refrigerator or cooler. Do not use if the cheese shows signs of spoilage.

PREPARATION AT HOME:

1. Combine dried ground beef, dried vegetables, paprika, and cayenne in a quart-size ziplock bag.
2. Package ramen and cream cheese separately.

PREPARATION ON THE TRAIL:

1. Add contents of vegetable-meat bag to pot along with 1½ cups of water and allow to rest for a few minutes.
2. Bring water to a boil and add ramen noodles, contents of seasoning packet, and cream cheese.
3. Stir until cream cheese is blended then serve.

REQUIRED EQUIPMENT ON THE TRAIL:
Cook pot

Marc Robinson, Canton, Michigan
Eagle Scout and Assistant Scoutmaster
Troop 854, Great Lakes Council

TIP:
See recipe for Great Lakes Ground Beef for instructions on dehydrating ground meats.

Servings: 1
Total Weight: About 5 ounces
Preparation Time on the Trail: ¼ hour
Challenge Level: Easy

Philadelphia Cheese Steak Tacos

PREPARATION AT HOME:

1. Dry sliced roast beef, chopped bell pepper, and chopped onion in a dehydrator.
2. Break dried beef into small pieces and place in a quart-size ziplock bag along with the dried bell pepper, dried onion, cayenne, and powdered cheese.
3. Carry soft taco shells separately.

PREPARATION ON THE TRAIL:

1. Add beef mix to water in a pot. Bring to a boil.
2. Reduce heat and simmer for about 10 minutes or until the beef has softened, adding more water if needed.
3. Divide beef mixture among the 4 taco shells then serve.

REQUIRED EQUIPMENT ON THE TRAIL:

Cook pot

Ken Spiegel, Farmingville, New York
Committee Member
Troop 80, Suffolk County Council

½ pound thinly sliced roast beef

1 bell pepper, chopped

1 onion, chopped

¼ teaspoon ground cayenne pepper

⅓ cup cheese powder

4 soft taco shells

¾ cup water, added on the trail

Option: A packet of cheese mix from a box of Kraft Macaroni & Cheese can be substituted for the dried powdered cheese. Retain the cheese in its packet for the trail.

Servings: 2
Total Weight: 10 ounces
Weight per Serving: 5 ounces
Preparation Time on the Trail: ¼ hour
Challenge Level: Moderate

Slim Jim's Pasta

½ cup Just Veggies brand freeze-dried vegetable mix

½ cup dried mushrooms, chopped into small pieces

2 tablespoons Nestle Nido whole milk powder

1 (4.8-ounce) package Knorr Pasta Sides Cheddar Broccoli

1 (1.8-ounce) package Slim Jim jerky

1 (3-ounce) brick cheddar cheese

3 cups water, added on the trail

Option: In place of the freeze-dried vegetable mix, a frozen vegetable mix from the grocer can be thawed and dried in a home food dehydrator for this recipe.

TIP:
Dried mushrooms can be found at larger grocery stores. Or fresh mushrooms are easy to dry in a home dehydrator.

Servings: 2–3
Total Weight: 13 ounces
Weight per Serving: About 6 ounces
Preparation Time on the Trail: ¼ hour
Challenge Level: Easy

PREPARATION AT HOME:

1. Combine dried vegetables, mushrooms, and milk powder in a quart-size ziplock bag.
2. Carry pasta package, Slim Jim, and cheese separately.

PREPARATION ON THE TRAIL:

1. Add vegetable mix to 3 cups water in a pot and bring to a boil.
2. To the pot, add pasta, stir, then reduce heat to a low boil until the pasta fully rehydrates.
3. Slice Slim Jim and cheese brick into small pieces and add to pot once pasta is cooked.
4. Stir often until cheese melts.

REQUIRED EQUIPMENT ON THE TRAIL:

Cook pot

Marc Robinson, Canton, Michigan
Eagle Scout and Assistant Scoutmaster
Troop 854, Great Lakes Council

Sunny Daze Rice

1 (6-ounce) package Uncle Ben's Country Inn Broccoli Rice au Gratin

1 (15-ounce) can mixed vegetables

1 (12-ounce) can Spam

2¼ cups water, added on the trail

PREPARATION AT HOME:

1. Remove rice grain and seasoning packet from rice package and place in a quart-size ziplock bag.
2. Carry cans of vegetables and Spam separately.

PREPARATION ON THE TRAIL:

1. Add rice and contents of seasoning packet to 2¼ cups water in a pot. Bring to boil.
2. Lower the heat, cover pot, and simmer for about 10 minutes or until the rice softens.
3. Drain vegetables and slice Spam into small cubes. Add to the pot.
4. Stir until heated through.

REQUIRED EQUIPMENT ON THE TRAIL:

Cook pot
Can opener

Option: A foil pouch of cooked chicken can be substituted for the Spam.

Scott Lane, South Vienna, Ohio
Assistant Scoutmaster
Troop 734, Simon Kenton Council

Pasta and beef is a hearty finish to the day.
CHRISTINE CONNERS

Servings: 3–4
Total Weight: 2¼ pounds
Weight per Serving: About 10 ounces
Preparation Time on the Trail: ½ hour
Challenge Level: Easy

Hot Cheap Dates

¼ cup chopped almonds

4 ounces goat cheese

8 ounces pitted whole deglet noor dates

1 (2-ounce) package precooked bacon

2 tablespoons brown sugar

¼ cup canola oil

Caution: Be careful when carrying any cheese on the trail by storing it buried in the cooler parts of your pack, using it soon after leaving the trailhead, and checking it carefully for spoilage before use. Some goat cheeses contain more salt than others or have protective rinds that will permit longer periods without refrigeration. Use discretion.

"I was first introduced to this recipe by a friend in Seattle. We both love it, and we've made several variations of it since. Dates are amazing when stuffed with nuts and cheeses, especially goat cheese such as Humboldt Fog or Spanish Manchego."

PREPARATION AT HOME:

1. Carry almonds, cheese, dates, and bacon separately and in their original packaging, if applicable.
2. Pack brown sugar in a quart-size heavy-duty ziplock bag.
3. Carry oil separately.

PREPARATION ON THE TRAIL:

1. In the 1-quart ziplock bag, combine chopped almonds and goat cheese with brown sugar. Knead well.
2. Cut a small corner from the bottom of the bag and squeeze mixture into the core of each of the pitted dates.
3. Slice bacon strips into halves. Wrap bacon around the dates and spear with toothpicks to hold together.
4. Heat oil in skillet and fry dates until the cheese appears to have melted. Don't burn the bottoms.

REQUIRED EQUIPMENT ON THE TRAIL:

Skillet
About 30 toothpicks

Curt "The Titanium Chef" White, Forks, Washington
Committee Member
Troop 1467, Chief Seattle Council

Servings: 6
Total Weight: 1 pound 1 ounce
Weight per Serving: About 3 ounces
Preparation Time on the Trail: ½ hour
Challenge Level: Moderate

Backwoods Pizza

"This is a favorite with our Scouts, and it's so simple to do. They always choose pizza over the freeze-dried meals."

6 soft taco tortillas

1 (5-ounce) packet Boboli pizza sauce

2 ounces pepperoni

3 (1-ounce) packages stick string cheese

1 tablespoon vegetable oil

Optional toppings: rehydrated dried mushrooms, tomatoes, onions, and olives

PREPARATION AT HOME:

1. Carry tortillas, pizza sauce packet, pepperoni, packaged cheese sticks, and oil separately.

PREPARATION ON THE TRAIL:

1. Tear cheese into strings.
2. Pour oil in pan and warm over low heat.
3. For each pizza, add 1 tortilla to the pan and about ⅓ of sauce and optional toppings followed by cheese strings from one of the sticks of cheese.
4. Cover with a second tortilla and fry "pizza" on each side until cheese melts.

REQUIRED EQUIPMENT ON THE TRAIL:

Skillet
Spatula

Judy Gratsch, Grand Blanc, Michigan
Assistant Scoutmaster
Troop 176, Tall Pine Council

Servings: 3
Total Weight: 14 ounces
Weight per Serving: About 5 ounces
Preparation Time on the Trail: ½ hour
Challenge Level: Easy

Spam and Pineapple

1 (12-ounce) can Spam

1 (8-ounce) can pineapple chunks

1 tablespoon butter

¼ cup brown sugar

Caution: Butter can be left at room temperature for 1 or 2 days, but after that, it will spoil rapidly.

"Christine is from Hawaii. She'll put pineapple on everything, given the chance, even backpacking food."—Tim

PREPARATION AT HOME:

1. Pack Spam and pineapple in their original cans.
2. Carry butter and brown sugar separately.

PREPARATION ON THE TRAIL:

1. Melt butter in pan. Add brown sugar and stir to blend.
2. Slice Spam into ½-inch-thick pieces then add to pan along with the pineapple and its juice.
3. Fry and flip Spam until it is lightly browned on both sides.

REQUIRED EQUIPMENT ON THE TRAIL:

Skillet
Can opener

Tim Conners, Statesboro, Georgia
Assistant Scoutmaster
Troop 340, Coastal Empire Council

Christine Conners, Statesboro, Georgia
Committee Member and Merit Badge Counselor
Troop 340, Coastal Empire Council

Servings: 3–4
Total Weight: 1½ pounds
Weight per Serving: About 7 ounces
Preparation Time on the Trail: ¼ hour
Challenge Level: Easy

Long Valley Logan Bread

"This recipe is said to have originated during the University of Alaska's expedition to Mount Logan in 1950. Since then, it has become a staple on many other 'expeditions,' both long and short."

3 cups whole-wheat flour
1 teaspoon salt
2 cups quick oats
1 cup wheat germ
½ cup Nestle Nido whole milk powder
1½ teaspoons baking powder
½ cup brown sugar
1 cup applesauce
4 eggs
1 cup maple syrup
¼ cup vegetable oil
1 cup chopped nuts (your choice)
1 cup chopped dates

PREPARATION AT HOME:

1. In a large bowl, combine flour, salt, oats, wheat germ, milk powder, baking powder, and brown sugar.
2. In a medium-size bowl, combine applesauce, eggs, syrup, and oil. Stir well.
3. Add contents of the second bowl to the first bowl and mix well.
4. Fold nuts and dates into the batter.
5. Spread dough into greased 9 x 13-inch pan.
6. Bake at 275°F for 1½ hours.
7. Allow to cool then cut into squares about 2 inches on a side.
8. Package for the trail in ziplock bags.

REQUIRED EQUIPMENT ON THE TRAIL:

None

TIP:
Logan bread is inherently durable but can be dried to further increase its longevity (and to reduce its weight a tad). To dry, slice the bread into pieces resembling biscotti and place on a cookie sheet. Set oven at its lowest temperature, keeping door slightly ajar, and dry the bread on the cookie sheet for about 2 hours. It will be very solid, but still tasty. Makes a great coffee dip.

Tim Conners, Statesboro, Georgia
Assistant Scoutmaster
Troop 340, Coastal Empire Council

Christine Conners, Statesboro, Georgia
Committee Member and Merit Badge Counselor
Troop 340, Coastal Empire Council

Servings: 24
Total Weight: 3½ pounds
Weight per Serving: About 2 ounces
Preparation Time on the Trail: None
Challenge Level: Easy

Glacier Park Garlic Biscuits

2 cups Heart Smart Bisquick baking mix

3 tablespoons Nestle Nido whole milk powder

2 tablespoons whole egg powder

2 teaspoons garlic salt

2 teaspoons Italian seasoning blend

¼ cup olive oil

1¼ cups water, added on the trail, plus additional for BakePacker

TIP: Baking takes more fuel and, occasionally, as in this case, a larger pot than the typical backpacking recipe calls for. When baking on the trail, be sure that your gear and fuel load are up to the task.

Servings: 4–5
Total Weight: 15 ounces
Weight per Serving: About 3 ounces
Preparation Time on the Trail: 1 hour
Challenge Level: Moderate

PREPARATION AT HOME:

1. Combine Bisquick, milk powder, and egg powder in a gallon-size heavy-duty ziplock bag.
2. Combine garlic salt, Italian seasoning, and olive oil in a small leak-proof plastic bottle and carry separately.

PREPARATION ON THE TRAIL:

1. Add 1¼ cups water to the bag of Bisquick mix and knead well.
2. Place BakePacker in pot and add water to top of the BakePacker grid.
3. Lay oven bag on the BakePacker grid with the top of the bag wide open.
4. Cut a large corner from the bottom of the Bisquick bag and squeeze contents into the open oven bag.
5. Loosely roll the top of the bag closed, but do not seal.
6. Cover pot and bring water to a boil for about 35 minutes, until dough appears cooked throughout.
7. Remove pot from heat and set oven bag aside to cool for a few minutes.
8. Remove bread from the bag and tear into individual servings.
9. Pour olive oil mix over top of bread or use as a dipping sauce.

REQUIRED EQUIPMENT ON THE TRAIL:

4-quart cook pot with lid
Standard-size (7⅜-inch) BakePacker
1 large-size (not "turkey-size") oven bag

Tim Conners, Statesboro, Georgia
Assistant Scoutmaster
Troop 340, Coastal Empire Council

Christine Conners, Statesboro, Georgia
Committee Member and Merit Badge Counselor
Troop 340, Coastal Empire Council

Bar Harbor Bannock Bread

¾ cup all-purpose flour

¾ cup whole-wheat flour

¼ cup Nestle Nido whole milk powder

2 teaspoons baking powder

1 tablespoon granulated sugar

2 tablespoons vegetable oil

1 cup water, added on the trail

Optional: honey condiment packets

PREPARATION AT HOME:

1. Combine flours, milk powder, baking powder, and sugar in a quart-size heavy-duty ziplock bag.
2. Carry oil separately.

PREPARATION ON THE TRAIL:

1. Warm oil in pan over medium-low heat.
2. Add 1 cup water to flour bag and knead well.
3. Once the oil is hot, cut a large corner from the bottom of the bag and squirt dough into pan. This can be done to make one large fry bread or several smaller biscuits.
4. Fry bread on each side for 5 to 10 minutes or until the bottoms become a golden brown and the inside rises and is fully baked.
5. Top with optional honey and serve.

REQUIRED EQUIPMENT ON THE TRAIL:

Skillet
Spatula

Jim "Cinnamonboy" Rausch, Ellsworth, Maine
Assistant Scoutmaster
Troop 86, Katahdin Area Council

TIP: Some backpacking stoves are nearly impossible to throttle to low flame levels. If your stove is one of those, be prepared for more pan work to keep the bread from burning.

Servings: 5–6
Total Weight: 12 ounces
Weight per Serving: About 2 ounces
Preparation Time on Trail: ½ hour
Challenge Level: Moderate

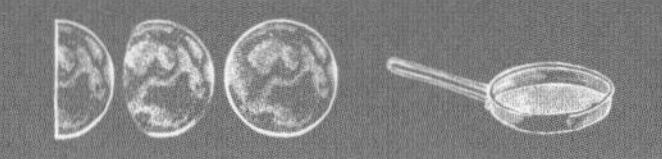

Chief Seattle Cornmeal Fry Biscuits

2 cups instant cornmeal

2 tablespoons dried minced onion

1 teaspoon baking powder

1 tablespoon garlic powder

¼ cup bacon bits

½ teaspoon salt

1 cup grated Parmesan cheese

¼ cup whole egg powder

¼ cup vegetable oil

2¼ cups water, added on the trail

PREPARATION AT HOME:

1. Combine cornmeal, dried onion, baking powder, garlic powder, bacon bits, salt, Parmesan, and egg powder in a gallon-size heavy-duty ziplock bag.
2. Carry oil separately.

PREPARATION ON THE TRAIL:

1. Add 2¼ cups water to cornmeal bag and knead into a uniform dough.
2. While the oil is heating in the pan, roll dough into golf ball-size balls and flatten between palms.
3. Fry biscuits until they are golden brown on each side.

REQUIRED EQUIPMENT ON THE TRAIL:

Skillet
Spatula

Curt "The Titanium Chef" White, Forks, Washington
Committee Member
Troop 1467, Chief Seattle Council

TIP:
Instant cornmeal can be found in the Hispanic foods section at the grocery store.

M-m-m-m, Cornmeal Fry Biscuits are cheesy and delicious. CHRISTINE CONNERS

Servings: 6–7
Total Weight: 1 pound 3 ounces
Weight per Serving: About 3 ounces
Preparation Time on the Trail: ½ hour
Challenge Level: Easy

Mojo Monkey Bread

2 cups Heart Smart Bisquick baking mix

3 tablespoons Nestle Nido whole milk powder

2 tablespoons whole egg powder

¼ cup brown sugar

¼ cup (½ standard stick) butter

2 teaspoons ground cinnamon

½ cup chopped pecans

1¼ cups water, added on the trail, plus additional for BakePacker

PREPARATION AT HOME:

1. Combine Bisquick, milk powder, and egg powder in a gallon-size heavy duty ziplock bag.
2. In a quart-size heavy-duty ziplock bag, combine brown sugar, butter, cinnamon, and pecans.

PREPARATION ON THE TRAIL:

1. Add 1¼ cups water to the bag of Bisquick mix and knead well.
2. Place BakePacker in pot and add water to top of the BakePacker grid.
3. Lay oven bag on the BakePacker grid with the top of the bag wide open.
4. Cut a large corner from the bottom of the Bisquick bag and squeeze contents into the open oven bag.
5. Loosely roll the top of the bag closed, but do not seal.
6. Cover pot and bring water to a boil for about 35 minutes, until dough appears cooked throughout.
7. Remove pot from heat and set oven bag aside to cool for a few minutes.
8. Set sealed bag of sugar-butter mix in the remaining hot water in the pot to fully melt the butter.
9. Remove bread from the bag and tear into pieces.
10. Carefully cut a small corner from bottom of the butter bag and squeeze contents onto the top of the bread.

REQUIRED EQUIPMENT ON THE TRAIL:

4-quart cook pot with lid
Standard-size (7⅜-inch) BakePacker
1 large-size (not "turkey-size") oven bag

Caution: Butter can remain at room temperature for 1 or 2 days, but after that, it will spoil rapidly. Plan to use fresh butter soon after leaving the trailhead.

TIP: Baking takes more fuel and, occasionally, as in this case, a larger pot than the typical backpacking recipe calls for. When baking on the trail, be sure that your gear and fuel load are up to the task.

Servings: 4–5
Total Weight: 1 pound 4 ounces
Weight per Serving: About 5 ounces
Preparation Time on the Trail: 1 hour
Challenge Level: Moderate

Tim Conners, Statesboro, Georgia
Assistant Scoutmaster
Troop 340, Coastal Empire Council

Christine Conners, Statesboro, Georgia
Committee Member and Merit Badge Counselor
Troop 340, Coastal Empire Council

 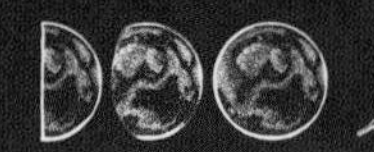   

Mango Madness Fruit Leather

1 (30-ounce) can mango puree/pulp, sweetened or unsweetened

PREPARATION AT HOME:

1. Pour mango puree onto parchment or plastic-lined dehydrator trays. Spread the puree as thinly as possible to produce more uniform drying.
2. Set dehydrator temperature to 135°F and dry until stickiness is gone, about 8 to 12 hours.
3. Place dried mango in a ziplock bag and keep refrigerated or frozen until ready to head to the trail.

REQUIRED EQUIPMENT ON THE TRAIL:
None

Tim Conners, Statesboro, Georgia
Assistant Scoutmaster
Troop 340, Coastal Empire Council

Christine Conners, Statesboro, Georgia
Committee Member and Merit Badge Counselor
Troop 340, Coastal Empire Council

TIP:
Mango puree is commonly found at Filipino and Indian grocers. It is also readily available online. If using sweetened pulp, be sure the sweetener is cane sugar and not high-fructose corn syrup. Corn syrup can make the leather sticky, impossible to fully dry.

Servings: 4
Total Weight: 9 ounces
Weight per Serving: About 2 ounces
Preparation Time on the Trail: None
Challenge Level: Easy

Mud

- ¼ cup old-fashioned oats
- ¼ cup nonfat milk powder
- ¼ cup sunflower seeds
- ¼ cup raisins
- ¼ cup chopped walnuts
- ¼ cup mini chocolate chips
- ½ cup peanut butter
- ½ cup honey

Option: Try peanut butter chips in place of chocolate chips.

PREPARATION AT HOME:

1. Mix all ingredients and place in a container for use on the trail.

PREPARATION ON THE TRAIL:

1. Eat straight from the container or use as a spread on crackers or bagels.

REQUIRED EQUIPMENT ON THE TRAIL:

None

Sherry Bennett, Rochester, New York
Former Den Leader and Merit Badge Counselor
Otetiana Council

Servings: 10
Total Weight: 1 pound 2 ounces
Weight per Serving: About 2 ounces
Preparation Time on the Trail: None
Challenge Level: Easy

Grunch

1 cup crunchy peanut butter

½ cup honey

½ cup finely crushed graham cracker crumbs

¼ cup nonfat milk powder

3 tablespoons ground cinnamon

1 tablespoon ground cloves

PREPARATION AT HOME:

1. Mix all ingredients and pack in a container for use on the trail.

PREPARATION ON THE TRAIL:

1. Eat straight from the container or use as a spread on crackers or bread.

REQUIRED EQUIPMENT ON THE TRAIL:

None

Sherry Bennett, Rochester, New York
Former Den Leader and Merit Badge Counselor
Otetiana Council

Servings: 10
Total Weight: 1 pound 2 ounces
Weight per Serving: About 2 ounces
Preparation Time on the Trail: None
Challenge Level: Easy

Spirit Lifters

"I like foods that you can look forward to, that lift your spirit when you're tired. This recipe goes a long way in doing that. Kind of like the feeling you get on a bitter cold, windy day, when someone puts a hot cup of tea in your hands."

½ cup whole-wheat flour
½ cup all-purpose flour
½ cup brown sugar
½ cup quick oats
¼ cup wheat germ
1 tablespoon grated orange rind
½ cup butter, softened
2 eggs
1 cup slivered almonds
¼ cup raisins
¼ cup flaked coconut
½ cup semisweet chocolate chips

PREPARATION AT HOME:

1. Preheat oven to 350°F.
2. In a large bowl, combine flours, brown sugar, oats, wheat germ, and orange rind.
3. Beat in the butter, eggs, almonds, raisins, coconut, and chocolate chips.
4. Line a 9 x 9-inch pan with parchment paper. Evenly pour in the batter.
5. Bake for 35 minutes.
6. Cool and cut into 16 bars then package for the trail.

REQUIRED EQUIPMENT ON THE TRAIL:

None

Sherry Bennett, Rochester, New York
Former Den Leader and Merit Badge Counselor
Otetiana Council

Servings: 16
Total weight: 1¾ pounds
Weight per Serving: About 2 ounces
Preparation Time on the Trail: None
Challenge Level: Easy

 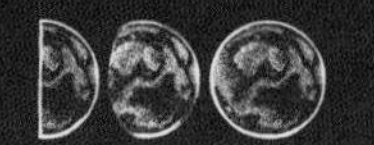 

Mount Fuji Rice Cakes

3 cups sweet rice flour

1¼ cups granulated sugar

1⅓ cups dried blueberries

3 eggs

¾ cup canola oil

1½ cups water

"Don't expect these rice cakes to resemble the bland, very-low-calorie versions found at the grocery store. The cakes from this recipe are a dense, durable, sweet-tasting treat."

PREPARATION AT HOME:

1. Preheat oven to 375°F.
2. In a large bowl, combine rice flour, sugar, and blueberries.
3. In a separate bowl, beat the eggs then stir in the canola oil and water.
4. Combine the wet ingredients with the dry and mix well.
5. Distribute batter among 24 cavities in muffin pans.
6. Bake for 30 minutes or until golden brown. A knife poked into the middle should come out clean.

REQUIRED EQUIPMENT ON THE TRAIL:

None

Tim Conners, Statesboro, Georgia
Assistant Scoutmaster
Troop 340, Coastal Empire Council

Christine Conners, Statesboro, Georgia
Committee Member and Merit Badge Counselor
Troop 340, Coastal Empire Council

Servings: 24
Total Weight: 3 pounds
Weight per Serving: 2 ounces
Preparation Time on the Trail: None
Challenge Level: Easy

Shake It! Pudding

PREPARATION AT HOME:

1. In a quart-size heavy-duty ziplock bag, combine pudding mix and milk powder.
2. Carry optional toppings separately.

PREPARATION ON THE TRAIL:

1. Pour 2 cups cold water into pudding bag. Seal tightly and knead to break up the clumps.
2. Shake pudding bag for about 5 minutes or until the pudding congeals.
3. Serve with optional toppings.

REQUIRED EQUIPMENT ON THE TRAIL:

None

Tim Conners, Statesboro, Georgia
Assistant Scoutmaster
Troop 340, Coastal Empire Council

Christine Conners, Statesboro, Georgia
Committee Member and Merit Badge Counselor
Troop 340, Coastal Empire Council

1 (3.4-ounce) package Jell-O instant pudding mix (your favorite flavor)

6 tablespoons Nestle Nido whole milk powder

Optional toppings: sprinkles, mini chocolate chips, freeze-dried bananas, or crushed cookies

2 cups cold water, added on the trail

TIP:
Be sure the pudding is in fact "instant." This recipe won't work with regular cook-and-serve pudding mix.

Servings: 3–4
Total Weight: 6 ounces
Weight per Serving: About 2 ounces
Preparation Time on the Trail: 5 minutes
Challenge Level: Easy

S'mores Gorp

1 (10-ounce) bag mini marshmallows

2 (19-ounce) bags M&Ms

1 (1-pound) package Golden Grahams cereal

1 (1-pound) container honey-roasted peanuts

PREPARATION AT HOME:

1. Combine all ingredients in a large bowl.
2. Subdivide into ziplock bags as required for your trip length and group size.

REQUIRED EQUIPMENT ON THE TRAIL:

None

Tracy Tuttle, Boise, Idaho
Den Leader
Pack 97, Ore-Ida Council

The fresh air west of New Army Pass, near the Pacific Crest Trail, makes a Scout hungry. *TIM CONNERS*

Servings: 27
Total Weight: About 5 pounds
Weight per Serving: About 3 ounces
Preparation Time on the Trail: None
Challenge Level: Easy

Galactic Pies

PREPARATION AT HOME:

1. In a bowl, combine milk powder, pudding mix, and coconut.
2. Divide the pudding mixture evenly between 2 quart-size heavy-duty ziplock bags.
3. Place 10 vanilla wafers into each of 2 separate small ziplock bags and crush.

PREPARATION ON THE TRAIL:

1. To prepare 2 servings, add 1 cup cold water to 1 bag of the pudding mix.
2. Seal and shake pudding bag vigorously until the mixture thickens. This may take a couple of minutes.
3. Add 1 bag of crushed wafers to the pudding bag and knead. Can be served straight from the bag.

REQUIRED EQUIPMENT ON THE TRAIL:

None

Tim Conners, Statesboro, Georgia
Assistant Scoutmaster
Troop 340, Coastal Empire Council

Christine Conners, Statesboro, Georgia
Committee Member and Merit Badge Counselor
Troop 340, Coastal Empire Council

⅔ cup nonfat milk powder

1 (3½-ounce) package instant vanilla pudding mix

1 cup shredded sweetened coconut

20 vanilla wafers

1 cup cold water per 2 servings, added on the trail

Servings: 4
Total Weight: 13 ounces
Weight per Serving: About 3 ounces
Preparation Time on the Trail: 5 minutes
Challenge Level: Easy

 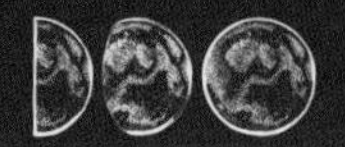 

Mossy Oak Banana Puddin'

⅔ cup nonfat milk powder

1 (3½-ounce) package banana cream instant pudding mix

20 vanilla wafers

1 cup dried banana chips

1 cup cold water per 2 servings, added on the trail

PREPARATION AT HOME:

1. In a bowl, combine milk powder with pudding mix. Divide the mixture evenly into each of 2 quart-size heavy-duty ziplock bags.
2. Crush vanilla wafers and banana chips into pieces, combine, and then evenly divide into each of 2 separate ziplock bags.

PREPARATION ON THE TRAIL:

1. To produce 2 servings, add 1 cup of cold water to 1 bag of the pudding-milk mix.
2. Seal and shake pudding bag vigorously for about 1 minute. The pudding will thicken within a couple of minutes.
3. Add the wafer-banana mix to the pudding bag and knead. Can be served straight from the bag.

REQUIRED EQUIPMENT ON THE TRAIL:

None

Tim Conners, Statesboro, Georgia
Assistant Scoutmaster
Troop 340, Coastal Empire Council

Christine Conners, Statesboro, Georgia
Committee Member and Merit Badge Counselor
Troop 340, Coastal Empire Council

Servings: 4
Total Weight: 12 ounces
Weight per Serving: 3 ounces
Preparation Time on the Trail: 5 minutes
Challenge Level: Easy

Trekker's Tapioca Pudding

PREPARATION AT HOME:

1. Combine tapioca, milk powder, salt, egg powder, and sugar in a quart-size ziplock bag.

PREPARATION ON THE TRAIL:

1. Place tapioca mix and 3 cups of water in a pot. Stir and let rest for 5 minutes.
2. Bring to a boil then remove from heat.
3. Allow to cool for about 10 minutes and serve warm.

REQUIRED EQUIPMENT ON THE TRAIL:

Cook pot

Tim Conners, Statesboro, Georgia
Assistant Scoutmaster
Troop 340, Coastal Empire Council

Christine Conners, Statesboro, Georgia
Committee Member and Merit Badge Counselor
Troop 340, Coastal Empire Council

½ cup Minute brand tapioca

½ cup Nestle Nido whole milk powder

¼ teaspoon salt

¼ cup whole egg powder

½ cup granulated sugar

3 cups water, added on the trail

Servings: 4–5
Total Weight: 10 ounces
Weight per Serving: About 2 ounces
Preparation Time on the Trail: ½ hour
Challenge Level: Easy

Backpacker's Rice Pudding

⅔ cup milk powder

1½ cups instant white rice

½ teaspoon ground cinnamon

½ teaspoon brown sugar

1 pinch nutmeg

1 (3.4-ounce) package vanilla instant pudding mix

1 cup raisins

1⅓ cups water per 2 servings, added on the trail

PREPARATION AT HOME:

1. Mix all dry ingredients in a bowl.
2. Evenly divide rice pudding mix into 2 quart-size ziplock bags. Each bag makes 2 servings.

PREPARATION AT CAMP:

1. For 2 servings (1 bag of pudding mix), bring 1⅓ cups of water to a boil.
2. Add rice pudding mix from a single bag to the pot and return to a light boil over medium heat. Stir.
3. Remove from stove, cover, and let stand for 5 minutes before serving.

REQUIRED EQUIPMENT ON THE TRAIL:

Cook pot

Joseph E. Brown, Huntsville, Alabama
District Commissioner
Korea District, Far East Council

Servings: 4
Total Weight: 1 pound
Weight per Serving: 4 ounces
Preparation Time on the Trail: ¼ hour
Challenge Level: Easy

Funky Fruit Soup

PREPARATION AT HOME:
1. Place pudding mix in a quart-size heavy-duty ziplock bag.
2. Carry dried fruit separately.

PREPARATION ON THE TRAIL:
1. Bring dried fruit to a boil in 3 cups of water. Reduce heat and simmer for about 10 minutes then remove from stove.
2. Add 1 cup water to the bag of pudding. Seal and shake well to remove any clumps.
3. Add pudding to fruit soup. Stir and serve.

REQUIRED EQUIPMENT ON THE TRAIL:
Cook pot

Tim Conners, Statesboro, Georgia
Assistant Scoutmaster
Troop 340, Coastal Empire Council

Christine Conners, Statesboro, Georgia
Committee Member and Merit Badge Counselor
Troop 340, Coastal Empire Council

1 (3.4-ounce) package cook-and-serve pudding mix (your favorite flavor)

1 pound dried fruit mix (your favorite blend)

4 cups water, added on the trail

Servings: 4–5
Total Weight: 1¼ pounds
Weight per Serving: About 4 ounces
Preparation Time on the Trail: ½ hour
Challenge Level: Easy

Muddy Swamp Brownies

1 cup granulated sugar

¼ cup whole egg powder

½ cup all-purpose flour

⅓ cup unsweetened cocoa powder

¼ teaspoon baking powder

¼ teaspoon salt

½ cup chopped walnuts or pecans

½ cup vegetable oil

2 tablespoons water, added on the trail

PREPARATION AT HOME:

1. Place sugar, egg powder, flour, cocoa powder, baking powder, salt, and nuts in a quart-size heavy-duty ziplock bag.
2. Carry oil separately.

PREPARATION ON THE TRAIL:

1. Add oil and 2 tablespoons water to the brownie mix bag and knead well.
2. Place BakePacker in pot and add water to top of the BakePacker grid.
3. Lay oven bag on the BakePacker grid with the top of the bag wide open.
4. Cut a large corner from the bottom of the brownie bag and squeeze contents into the open oven bag.
5. Loosely roll the top of the bag closed, but do not seal.
6. Cover pot and bring water to a boil for about 25 minutes. Serve warm.

REQUIRED EQUIPMENT ON THE TRAIL:

Cook pot with lid
Ultralight (5¾-inch) BakePacker
1 large-size (not "turkey-size") oven bag

TIP: Be sure the BakePacker fits inside of your cook pot before heading for the trail.

Tim Conners, Statesboro, Georgia
Assistant Scoutmaster
Troop 340, Coastal Empire Council

Christine Conners, Statesboro, Georgia
Committee Member and Merit Badge Counselor
Troop 340, Coastal Empire Council

Servings: 4–5
Total Weight: 1 pound 1 ounce
Weight per Serving: About 4 ounces
Preparation Time on the Trail: ½ hour
Challenge Level: Easy

Muir Woods Apple Crisp

"Climb the Mountains and get their good tidings."
—John Muir

¼ cup brown sugar

½ cup old-fashioned oats

1 teaspoon ground cinnamon

1 (5-ounce) package dried apples

¾ cup water, added on the trail

PREPARATION AT HOME:

1. In a quart-size ziplock bag, combine brown sugar, oats, and cinnamon.
2. Retain apples in their original packaging and carry separately.

PREPARATION ON THE TRAIL:

1. Place apples in ¾ cup of water and boil until they become tender. The apples should absorb most of the water.
2. Add oat mix to the apples in the pot and stir.

REQUIRED EQUIPMENT ON THE TRAIL:

Cook pot

Tim Conners, Statesboro, Georgia
Assistant Scoutmaster
Troop 340, Coastal Empire Council

Christine Conners, Statesboro, Georgia
Committee Member and Merit Badge Counselor
Troop 340, Coastal Empire Council

Hard backpacking calls for hard snacking! *TIM CONNERS*

Servings: 2
Total Weight: 9 ounces
Weight per Serving: About 5 ounces
Preparation Time on the Trail: ¼ hour
Challenge Level: Easy

Chocolate Raspberry Indulgence

1 (3½-ounce) package Jell-O Cook & Serve chocolate pudding mix

⅔ cup nonfat milk powder

1 ounce Just Raspberries brand freeze-dried raspberries

2 cups water, added on the trail

"This recipe recommends the use of a 'heat disperser' on those stoves that tend to scorch foods while cooking. We made our own lightweight version from the top of a large (3-pound) can of coffee. We removed the top using a smooth-edge can opener, one that cuts just below the rim, leaving a safe, non-jagged edge."

PREPARATION AT HOME:

1. Each item can be carried separately. Or the pudding mix and milk powder can be combined in a quart-size ziplock bag and the dried raspberries carried separately.

PREPARATION ON THE TRAIL:

1. Combine 2 cups of water with the milk powder and pudding mix in a pot.
2. Heat until the mixture comes to a full boil, stirring constantly. It is helpful to use a heat disperser between the pot and some stoves to minimize scorching. Remove from heat.
3. Divide the freeze-dried raspberries between two or three bowls or cups.
4. Pour the cooked chocolate pudding over the raspberries.
5. Serve warm or cold. If not eaten immediately, cover or close the bag to prevent a crust from forming.

REQUIRED EQUIPMENT ON THE TRAIL:

Cook pot
Heat disperser (if stove prone to scorching)

Ken Harbison, Rochester, New York
Former Boy Scout and Master Tester for *The Scout's Outdoor Cookbook*
Washington Trail Council

Servings: 2–3
Total Weight: 7 ounces
Weight per Serving: About 3 ounces
Preparation Time on the Trail: ¼ hour
Challenge Level: Moderate

Dirty Socks Peach Cobbler

"It really does look like dirty socks once it's finished cooking, but it tastes great."

1 (15-ounce) can sliced peaches in heavy syrup

½ cup Bisquick baking mix

¼ cup granulated sugar

¼ cup brown sugar

¼ teaspoon ground cinnamon

Vegetable oil for greasing skillet (if not using a nonstick pan)

½ cup water, added on the trail

PREPARATION AT HOME:

1. Drain peaches and cut into thin slices.
2. Dry peaches on a parchment or plastic-lined dehydrator tray then place in a small ziplock bag.
3. Place the remainder of the dry ingredients into a quart-size heavy-duty ziplock bag, and shake until mixed.
4. If your skillet is not nonstick, pack a little oil separately to grease the skillet on the trail.

PREPARATION ON THE TRAIL:

1. If not using a nonstick pan, grease the pan with oil.
2. Pour ¼ cup water along with the peaches into pan.
3. Stir, bringing peaches to a boil, then reduce heat.
4. Add ¼ cup water to the bag containing the Bisquick mix then knead.
5. Cut a large corner from the bottom of the bag and squeeze the dough mixture onto the peaches.
6. Scramble the mixture in the pan until the batter is fully cooked.

REQUIRED EQUIPMENT ON THE TRAIL:

Skillet

Tim Conners, Statesboro, Georgia
Assistant Scoutmaster
Troop 340, Coastal Empire Council

Christine Conners, Statesboro, Georgia
Committee Member and Merit Badge Counselor
Troop 340, Coastal Empire Council

Servings: 2
Total Weight: 9 ounces
Weight per Serving: About 5 ounces
Preparation Time on the Trail: ½ hour
Challenge Level: Easy

Switchback Smoothie

2 cups almond milk

½ cup honey

1 (16-ounce) bag frozen blueberries, thawed

1 (16-ounce) bag frozen fruit blend (such as strawberries, pineapple, etc.), thawed

2 bananas

2 tablespoons lemon juice

1 cup water per serving, added on the trail

Option: The dried fruit leather itself is very tasty and can be eaten as is.

"Smoothies are packed with good things for your body and they taste fantastic. If you are new to smoothies, be advised that they can be addicting. With a blender and a dehydrator, you already have all the kitchen tools you need to make a durable, portable, and great-tasting version of this wonderful drink. Carry extra to help you up those final switchbacks."

PREPARATION AT HOME:

1. Combine almond milk, honey, thawed fruit, bananas, and lemon juice together in a blender and puree.
2. Spread about 1 cup of mixture evenly over each of 7 parchment or plastic-lined dehydrator trays. Dry at about 135°F.
3. Remove the leather once it is no longer sticky to the touch.
4. Each tray produces 1 serving. Store each serving in a separate small ziplock bag.

PREPARATION ON THE TRAIL:

1. Tear 1 serving of leather into very small pieces and place in a wide-mouth bottle containing 1 cup cold water.
2. Allow mixture to dissolve for about 30 minutes, periodically shaking vigorously to help speed the process.

REQUIRED EQUIPMENT ON THE TRAIL:

Wide-mouth water bottle

Tim Conners, Statesboro, Georgia
Assistant Scoutmaster
Troop 340, Coastal Empire Council

Christine Conners, Statesboro, Georgia
Committee Member and Merit Badge Counselor
Troop 340, Coastal Empire Council

Servings: 7
Total Weight: 14 ounces
Weight per Serving: 2 ounces
Preparation Time on the Trail: ½ hour
Challenge Level: Easy

Whopper Malt Bribe

"This is one of those recipes, not designed with health in mind, but solely intended to move feet from Point A to Point B when they otherwise don't want to. When it's on the dessert menu, you just might be able to use Whopper Malt Bribe to coerce your feet into taking those last few thousand steps of the day."

1 cup crushed Whoppers

1 cup Ovaltine chocolate malt mix

1 cup nonfat milk powder

Option: Works well as a hot drink too.

PREPARATION AT HOME:

1. Crush the Whoppers and combine all ingredients in a quart-size ziplock bag.

PREPARATION ON THE TRAIL:

1. To prepare 1 serving, add ½ cup dry mix to 1 cup cold water.
2. Stir and serve.

REQUIRED EQUIPMENT ON THE TRAIL:

None

Tim Conners, Statesboro, Georgia
Assistant Scoutmaster
Troop 340, Coastal Empire Council

Christine Conners, Statesboro, Georgia
Committee Member and Merit Badge Counselor
Troop 340, Coastal Empire Council

Servings: 6
Total Weight: 9 ounces
Weight per Serving: About 2 ounces
Preparation Time on the Trail: Less than ¼ hour
Challenge Level: Easy

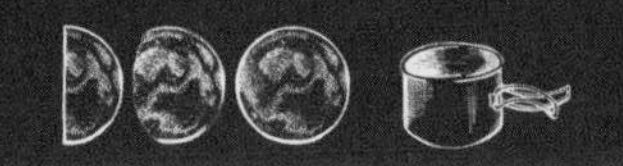

Cowboy Coffee

½ cup coffee grounds, medium grind

1 quart cold water

Options: Experiment with different grinds, roasts, strengths, and boiling times to find your perfect cup of coffee.

"Our friend and former Scouter, Pete Fish, taught us how to make cowboy coffee on the trail. We've dabbled with his original recipe over the years, adapting it to camp and to larger groups. We've found cowboy coffee to be remarkably resilient against variations in cooking. Even when it's over-boiled, it's still pretty darn good."

PREPARATION AT HOME:

1. Package ground coffee for the trail in a small ziplock bag.

PREPARATION ON THE TRAIL:

1. Over cold water in a pot, float coffee grounds to form a thick mat.
2. Bring water to a boil momentarily then remove from heat.
3. Add a splash of cold water to settle any grounds that remain floating on the surface.
4. Carefully scoop coffee from the top of liquid to avoid disturbing the settled grounds, unless you like the coffee chewy (it's actually not bad that way).

REQUIRED EQUIPMENT ON THE TRAIL:

Cook pot

TIP:
As any gardener knows, coffee grounds make a great soil amendment; so burying used grinds in a proper cat hole should pose no issue to most local environments along the trail. Hike friendly, and do not scatter used grinds over the top of the ground. And be prepared to pack the waste out in sensitive areas.

Tim Conners, Statesboro, Georgia
Assistant Scoutmaster
Troop 340, Coastal Empire Council

Christine Conners, Statesboro, Georgia
Committee Member and Merit Badge Counselor
Troop 340, Coastal Empire Council

Servings: 4 (about 6–7 ounces each)
Total Weight: About 2 ounces
Weight per Serving: Less than 1 ounce
Preparation Time: Less than ¼ hour
Challenge Level: Easy

Venture Crew Hot Cocoa Mix

1½ cups unsweetened cocoa powder

1½ cups Nestle Nido whole milk powder

1 cup powdered nondairy creamer

2 cups powdered sugar

1 cup water per serving, added on the trail

PREPARATION AT HOME:

1. Combine all dry ingredients in a gallon-size heavy-duty ziplock bag.

PREPARATION ON THE TRAIL:

1. Bring water to boil, 1 cup for each serving.
2. Add 3 tablespoons cocoa powder mix to every 1 cup hot water.
3. Stir briskly and serve.

REQUIRED EQUIPMENT ON THE TRAIL:

Cook pot

Gerry Garges, Austin, Texas
Adviser
Crew 513, Capitol Area Council

TIP:
Adjusting ingredients to personalize sweetness, creaminess, or chocolate content will make this a true favorite.

Servings: 32
Total Weight: 1½ pounds
Weight per Serving: Less than 1 ounce
Preparation Time on the Trail: Less than ¼ hour
Challenge Level: Easy

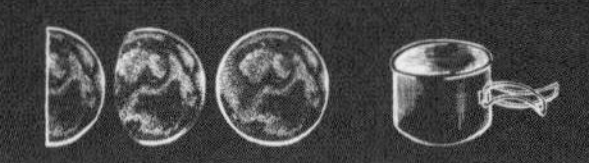

Mai Chai Tea

2 tablespoons Nestle Nido whole milk powder

2 heaping teaspoons dried honey granules

1 dash ground nutmeg

1 dash ground cinnamon

1 chai tea bag (2 bags, if you like stronger tea)

1½ cups water per serving, added on the trail

Option: Granulated sugar can be substituted for the honey granules.

"This hot tea drink evolved as I did more climbing and camping in the snow. It is very similar to sherpa climbing tea, but a bit spicier and great on winter camping trips. I generally use two tea bags, because I like it strong. 'Mai' in Japanese means 'Dance,' so Mai Chai is a dance of satisfaction after a long day on the trail."

PREPARATION AT HOME:

1. Combine milk powder, honey granules, nutmeg, and cinnamon in a small ziplock bag.
2. Carry tea bag separately.

PREPARATION ON THE TRAIL:

1. Bring 1½ cups water to a boil. Add tea bag and let steep for 3 to 5 minutes.
2. Add powdered milk mix, stir, and serve hot.

REQUIRED EQUIPMENT ON THE TRAIL:
Cook pot

Curt "The Titanium Chef" White, Forks, Washington
Committee Member
Troop 1467, Chief Seattle Council

Bitter cold is no match for hot tea and a warm bag! *CURT WHITE*

Servings: 1
Total Weight: About 1 ounce
Preparation Time on the Trail: ¼ hour
Challenge Level: Easy

Shawnee Sage Tea

"This recipe is named for the Shawnee Trail, a beautiful 46-mile loop in the tree-covered hill country of south-central Ohio, where Tim cut his teeth on long-distance hiking."

¼ cup granulated sugar

2 standard-size bags black tea

2 heaping tablespoons dried whole sage leaves

4 cups water, added on the trail

Option: For a delicious alternative, 2 tablespoons of dried whole mint or peppermint leaves can be substituted for the sage.

PREPARATION AT HOME:

1. Package ingredients separately for the trail.

PREPARATION ON THE TRAIL:

1. Bring 4 cups water to a boil, then add sugar. Doing so in this order helps to keep the tea clear.
2. Immediately remove pot from heat.
3. Add tea bags and sage leaves to the hot water. Let steep for several minutes before serving.

REQUIRED EQUIPMENT ON THE TRAIL:

Cook pot

TIP:
If the sage leaves are grown fresh, do not water the plant for at least 2 days prior to picking the leaves.

Tim Conners, Statesboro, Georgia
Assistant Scoutmaster
Troop 340, Coastal Empire Council

Christine Conners, Statesboro, Georgia
Committee Member and Merit Badge Counselor
Troop 340, Coastal Empire Council

Servings: 2
Total Weight: 2 ounces
Weight per Serving: 1 ounce
Preparation Time on the Trail: ¼ hour
Challenge Level: Easy

Jammin' Jell-O Juice

1 (3-ounce) box Jell-O gelatin (your favorite flavor)

2 cups water, added on the trail

PREPARATION AT HOME:

1. Remove Jell-O packet from box and place in a small ziplock bag.

PREPARATION ON THE TRAIL:

1. Bring water to a boil. Add Jell-O.
2. Stir and serve.

REQUIRED EQUIPMENT ON THE TRAIL:

Cook pot

Tim Conners, Statesboro, Georgia
Assistant Scoutmaster
Troop 340, Coastal Empire Council

Christine Conners, Statesboro, Georgia
Committee Member and Merit Badge Counselor
Troop 340, Coastal Empire Council

Servings: 2
Total Weight: 3 ounces
Weight per Serving: Less than 2 ounces
Preparation Time on the Trail: Less than ¼ hour
Challenge Level: Easy

Wassail! Backpacking-Style

"Many of my Scouts heard of 'wassail' from the holiday songs, but very few had ever tried it. I have roots in England and prepared traditional versions of it with fresh fruit. So I set out to devise a version that was lightweight and easy to prepare along the trail. This recipe is fun to make. You might even find yourself singing the wassailing song too."

PREPARATION AT HOME:

1. In a small ziplock bag, combine orange drink mix, allspice, nutmeg, cinnamon, ginger, and cloves.
2. Carry cider packets, condiment packets, and optional cinnamon sticks separately.

PREPARATION ON THE TRAIL:

1. Pour 1 packet of apple cider mix into each of two mugs.
2. Evenly divide the powdered ingredients from the ziplock bag into each mug.
3. Pour 1 cup boiling water into each mug.
4. Add honey and lemon juice to each mug, stirring to combine.
5. Cover mugs and let rest 2 or 3 minutes to give the spices time to bloom.
6. Stir well. Add more hot water if the drink is too strong for your liking.
7. Add optional cinnamon sticks then give a toast to good health and friends.

REQUIRED EQUIPMENT ON THE TRAIL:

Cook pot

Curt "The Titanium Chef" White, Forks, Washington
Committee Member
Troop 1467, Chief Seattle Council

2 tablespoons orange drink mix

1 dash ground allspice

1 dash ground nutmeg

1 dash ground cinnamon

1 dash ground ginger

1 dash ground cloves

2 spiced apple cider packets

2 condiment packets honey

1 condiment packet lemon juice

Optional: cinnamon sticks

2 cups water, added on the trail

Option: Other sweeteners can be substituted, but wassail tastes best with honey.

TIP: Condiment packets are available in bulk from online retailers, and honey can also be purchased online in crystalline or powdered form. See Appendix B.

Servings: 2
Total Weight: 4 ounces
Weight per Serving: 2 ounces
Preparation Time on the Trail: ¼ hour
Challenge Level: Easy

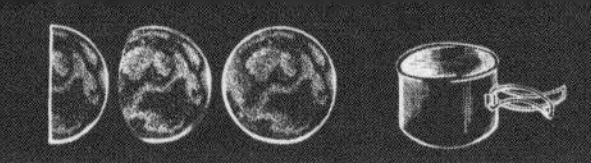

Panamint Peppermint Cooler

1 (4-ounce) package cherry-flavored sweetened Kool-Aid mix

1 (5-ounce) package lemonade-flavored sweetened Kool-Aid mix

1 (20-bag) box Celestial Seasonings peppermint herbal tea

4 cups water per serving, added on the trail

"This drink has the most amazing sequence of aftertastes, all of them intriguing. It starts with the sharp hit of the mint and then smoothly rolls into a series of sweet, fruity nuances. The large serving size makes it great for rehydrating."

PREPARATION AT HOME:

1. Combine cherry and lemonade flavored Kool-Aid mixes in a small ziplock bag.
2. Carry tea bags separately.

PREPARATION ON THE TRAIL:

1. To prepare 1 large serving, bring 2 cups water to a boil. Remove pot from heat.
2. Add 4 tea bags to the hot water and let steep for 6 minutes before removing.
3. While the water is still hot, add ¼ cup Kool-Aid mix and stir until dissolved.
4. Allow water to cool, then add 2 more cups cold water.
5. Pour into a 1-quart water bottle for extended enjoyment.

REQUIRED EQUIPMENT ON THE TRAIL:

Cook pot
1-quart water bottle

Tim Conners, Statesboro, Georgia
Assistant Scoutmaster
Troop 340, Coastal Empire Council

Christine Conners, Statesboro, Georgia
Committee Member and Merit Badge Counselor
Troop 340, Coastal Empire Council

Servings: 5
Total Weight: 12 ounces
Weight per Serving: About 2 ounces
Preparation Time on the Trail: ½ hour
Challenge Level: Easy

Appendix A

COMMON MEASUREMENT CONVERSIONS

United States Volumetric Conversions

1 smidgen	1/32 teaspoon
1 pinch	1/16 teaspoon
1 dash	1/8 teaspoon
3 teaspoons	1 tablespoon
48 teaspoons	1 cup
2 tablespoons	1/8 cup
4 tablespoons	1/4 cup
5 tablespoons + 1 teaspoon	1/3 cup
8 tablespoons	1/2 cup
12 tablespoons	3/4 cup
16 tablespoons	1 cup
1 ounce	2 tablespoons
4 ounces	1/2 cup
8 ounces	1 cup
5/8 cup	1/2 cup + 2 tablespoons
7/8 cup	3/4 cup + 2 tablespoons
2 cups	1 pint
2 pints	1 quart
1 quart	4 cups
4 quarts	1 gallon
1 gallon	128 ounces

Note: Dry and fluid volumes are equivalent for teaspoon, tablespoon, and cup.

International Metric System Conversions

Volume and Weight

United States	Metric
¼ teaspoon	1.25 milliliters
½ teaspoon	2.50 milliliters
¾ teaspoon	3.75 milliliters
1 teaspoon	5 milliliters
1 tablespoon	15 milliliters
1 ounce (volume)	30 milliliters
¼ cup	60 milliliters
½ cup	120 milliliters
¾ cup	180 milliliters
1 cup	240 milliliters
1 pint	0.48 liter
1 quart	0.95 liter
1 gallon	3.79 liters
1 ounce (weight)	28 grams
1 pound	0.45 kilogram

Temperature

Degrees F	Degrees C
175	80
200	95
225	105
250	120
275	135
300	150
325	165
350	175
375	190
400	205
425	220
450	230
475	245
500	260

British, Canadian, and Australian Conversions

1 teaspoon (Britain, Canada, Australia)	approx. 1 teaspoon (United States)
1 tablespoon (Britain, Canada)	approx. 1 tablespoon (United States)
1 tablespoon (Australia)	1.35 tablespoons (United States)
1 ounce (Britain, Canada, Australia)	0.96 ounce (United States)
1 gill (Britain)	5 ounces (Britain, Canada, Australia)
1 cup (Britain)	10 ounces (Britain, Canada, Australia)
1 cup (Britain)	9.61 ounces (United States)
1 cup (Britain)	1.20 cups (United States)
1 cup (Canada, Australia)	8.45 ounces (United States)
1 cup (Canada, Australia)	1.06 cups (United States)
1 pint (Britain, Canada, Australia)	20 ounces (Britain, Canada, Australia)
1 Imperial gallon (Britain)	1.20 gallons (United States)
1 pound (Britain, Canada, Australia)	1 pound (United States)

Equivalent Measures*

16 ounces water	1 pound
2 cups vegetable oil	1 pound
2 cups or 4 sticks butter	1 pound
2 cups granulated sugar	1 pound
3½ to 4 cups unsifted confectioners' sugar	1 pound
2¼ cups packed brown sugar	1 pound
4 cups sifted flour	1 pound
3½ cups unsifted whole wheat flour	1 pound
8–10 egg whites	1 cup
12–14 egg yolks	1 cup
1 whole lemon, squeezed	3 tablespoons juice
1 whole orange, squeezed	⅓ cup juice

* Approximate

Drying Conversions*

Undried Item	Dried Volume	Dried Weight
1 tablespoon fresh herbs	1 teaspoon	less than 1 ounce
1 tablespoon mustard	1 teaspoon	less than 1 ounce
1 garlic clove, pressed	⅛ teaspoon powder	less than 1 ounce
1 pound frozen peas	1 cup	4 ounces
1 pound cooked and sliced carrots	½ cup	2 ounces
1 pound boiled and sliced potatoes	1½ cups	4 ounces
1 pound diced onions	1 cup	1 ounce
1 pound frozen French-sliced green beans	2 cups	1½ ounces
1 pound diced celery	⅓ cup	½ ounce
1 pound sliced fresh mushrooms	2½ cups	1 ounce
1 pound fresh green bell pepper	¾ cup	1½ ounces
1 pound fresh jalapeño peppers	1⅓ cups	1 ounce
1 pound frozen mixed vegetables	¾ cup	3½ ounces
1 15-ounce can mixed vegetables	½ cup	1½ ounces
1 6-ounce can medium diced olives	½ cup	1 ounce
1 15-ounce can pinto beans	1 cup	2½ ounces

Undried Item	Dried Volume	Dried Weight
1 15-ounce can black beans	1 cup	2½ ounces
1 15-ounce can kidney beans	1¼ cups	3½ ounces
1 pound steamed and chopped zucchini	⅓ cup	½ ounce
1 pound frozen sliced broccoli	1 cup	1 ounce
1 pound sliced Roma tomatoes	1 cup	1 ounce
1 6-ounce can tomato paste	Leather roll	1½ ounces
1 pound salsa	½ cup	½ ounce
1 pound sliced apples	1½ cups	3 ounces
1 pound sliced bananas	1½ cups	4 ounces
1 20-ounce can diced pineapple	¾ cup	2 ounces
1 pound trimmed watermelon	1 cup	1 ounce
1 pound frozen cherries	½ cup	2 ounces
1 cup whole milk	½ cup powdered	2 ounces

* Volumes and weights may vary slightly from those shown here due to a variety of factors, including brand selection, depth of cut, dehydrating method, or equipment.

Appendix B

SOURCES OF EQUIPMENT AND SUPPLIES

AlpineAire
www.alpineaire.com
A good source for freeze-dried, ready-to-eat instant meals, AlpineAire's products are available through outfitters as well as at their online store.

Amazon
www.amazon.com
It's well known that Amazon sells an enormous array of products. But it might come as a surprise nevertheless that it also hosts a very large number of vendors selling exotic food ingredients difficult to find in your local grocery store. Check out Amazon if you're stumped finding an ingredient.

Asian Food Grocer
www.asianfoodgrocer.com
A wide selection of difficult-to-find Asian ingredients, including dried tofu, fish, and mushrooms, are available at Asian Grocer.

Backpacker's Pantry
www.backpackerspantry.com
Backpacker's Pantry is a well-known brand name at outdoor retailers, but their online store is also a very good source of freeze-dried meals as well as single-serving condiments like peanut butter, salsa, and jelly. Backpacker's Pantry also carries a selection of organic products.

Barry Farm Foods
www.barryfarm.com
Barry Farm offers an amazing selection of dried ingredients, including foods you might not believe could even be dried, such as cheese, sour cream, and yogurt.

Bass Pro Shops
www.basspro.com
Bass Pro is a nationwide retailer that stocks a range of outdoor gear appropriate for the trail. The Bass Pro stores are a good place to go to actually examine gear firsthand.

Boy Scout Catalog
www.scoutstuff.org
BSA Supply carries an assortment of handy gear for backpacking and trail cooking, including equipment for larger group settings. Check out their website for the full catalog.

Bulk Foods
www.bulkfoods.com
Here you'll find an enormous selection of dried fruits, spices, grains, and nuts sold in a variety of sizes and quantities.

Cabela's
www.cabelas.com
This retailer specializes as a hunting and fishing outfitter but also carries a nice selection of kitchen gear for the trail. Cabela's has dozens of large retail stores located throughout the United States and Southern Canada.

CampingMaxx
www.campingmaxx.com
CampingMaxx buys large quantities of outdoor camping and backpacking products at discount and passes along the savings to its customers.

Their catalog includes cooking gear and freeze-dried meals, and the equipment is particularly suited for large group purchases or for those on a limited budget.

Campmor
www.campmor.com
Campmor's online catalog has one of the most comprehensive selections of gear available anywhere for backpacking and cooking on the trail.

Eden Foods
www.edenfoods.com
An interesting array of Japanese foods can be found at Eden, including dried tofu, seaweed, spices, and mushrooms, as well as exotic and organic bulk goods.

Emergency Essentials
www.beprepared.com
A good source of dried goods sold in bulk, including whole egg powder and even meals-ready-to-eat (MRE's).

Fantastic Foods
www.fantasticfoods.com
A culinary voyage across continents and cultures, Fantastic Foods' internet store offers many dried products useful for backpacking, such as refried beans, falafel, hummus, and tabouli mixes.

Harmony House Foods
www.harmonyhousefoods.com
Harmony House is a great source for a large selection of dried vegetables and fruits in bulk.

Harvest Foodworks

www.harvestfoodworks.com

A wide range of freeze-dried and dehydrated meals for the outdoors can be found at Harvest Foodworks.

Just Tomatoes Etc.

www.justtomatoes.com

A wonderful source for individual bulk freeze-dried vegetables and fruits, Just Tomatoes doesn't offer just tomatoes. Their products are so tasty, you can eat them dry, right out of the bag.

King Arthur Flour

www.kingarthurflour.com

Popular at the grocer, King Arthur Flour is available at an online retail store that also offers a diverse selection of difficult-to-find ingredients, including whole egg powder, dried cheese, whole milk powder, and more.

Mountain Equipment Co-op

www.mec.ca

MEC is a large Canadian cooperative specializing in outdoor gear via an extensive online catalog and through more than a dozen retail stores located across Canada.

Mountain House

www.mtnhse.com

Mountain House is well-known at outdoor retailers for their freeze-dried meals, but online, they also offer a good selection of discounted bulk dried items such as vegetables, eggs, and premade entrees.

My Spicer

www.myspicer.com

An enormous selection of exotic dried vegetables and spices from around the world can be found at My Spicer.

PackitGourmet

www.packitgourmet.com

PackitGourmet stocks a large and unique selection of items with the backpacker in mind, including restaurant condiment packets in smaller lots and powdered citrus drinks.

REI

www.rei.com

REI is a membership cooperative that carries a large array of trail gear and freeze-dried foods online but also retails through dozens of superstores located throughout the United States, providing the opportunity to see before you buy. Be prepared to be bitten by the backpacking bug once you step foot in an REI.

Sport Chalet

www.sportchalet.com

Sport Chalet is a major outdoor recreation retailer in the Southwest United States. Like REI, this is an excellent place to go to see backpacking gear in general, and trail kitchen equipment and freeze-dried foods in particular, firsthand.

SunOrganic Farm

www.sunorganic.com

This retailer carries a good selection of organic dried fruits and vegetables as well as seasonings, beans, nuts, and sprouting seeds.

Suttons Bay Trading Company

www.suttonsbayspices.com

Suttons Bay Trading offers a large selection of dried fruit and vegetables, including an interesting assortment of flavored powders such as horseradish, soy sauce, yogurt, and even honey, which is impossible to dry in a home dehydrator.

Appendix C

ADDITIONAL READING AND RESOURCES

Books and Periodicals

***Backpacking*, Merit Badge Series, Boy Scouts of America**

Foundational skills are thoroughly covered in this popular booklet for Scouts earning their Backpacking Merit Badge. A working knowledge of trail cookery skills is an essential component of backpacking, and this topic is given detailed coverage, along with a list of challenging cooking-related requirements.

Cook's Illustrated* and *Cook's Country

www.cooksillustrated.com and www.cookscountry.com

These outstanding periodicals from America's Test Kitchen turn common recipes into wonderful re-creations but with a minimum amount of effort. Along the way, the reader learns how and why the recipes work. *Cook's Illustrated* explores fewer dishes but in more detail than *Cook's Country,* its sister publication, which comes in a larger format and full color. These are magazines for the home kitchen. But what you'll learn indoors will prove invaluable on the trail.

***Cooking*, Merit Badge Series, Boy Scouts of America**

Scouts interested in outdoor cuisine will naturally want to pursue the Cooking Merit Badge on their way to Eagle. This booklet addresses the basics of indoor and outdoor cooking, food safety and nutrition, and careers in the food service industry. Detailed Cooking Merit Badge requirements are included.

FalconGuides/Globe Pequot Press

www.falcon.com

FalconGuides is the top outdoor recreation book publisher in the country with an extensive catalog of books for nearly every outdoor activity, covering most states and geographical regions in the United States as well as many of the most popular National Parks.

***Lipsmackin' Backpackin'*, Tim and Christine Conners, Globe Pequot Press**

This book contains over 150 trail recipes from dozens of skilled backpackers from across the United States. *Lipsmackin' Backpackin'* is a good resource for recipes suitable for any type of trek, but especially those designed for durability on long-distance trips spanning more than a few days. Included with each recipe is a breakdown of key nutrients per serving.

***Lipsmackin' Vegetarian Backpackin'*, Christine and Tim Conners, Globe Pequot Press**

A younger sibling to its brother, *Lipsmackin' Backpackin'*, *Lipsmackin' Vegetarian* is also filled with recipes well-suited for backpacking trips of longer duration. But, as the title suggests, all the recipes are meatless. "Vegetarian" doesn't have to mean "bland," of course, and the more than 150 tasty recipes in this book from over fifty experienced backpackers attest to that. This is a good resource for expanding your list of reliable, durable, and tasty trail recipes.

***On Food and Cooking: The Science and Lore of the Kitchen*, Harold McGee, Scribner**

This is an excellent resource for understanding the science behind cooking. When chefs decipher why recipes work the way they do, they become much more effective at adapting recipes in a pinch or creating new ones on the fly. Be forewarned. This is not a cookbook, much less an outdoor cookbook. But if science interests you, this book will too.

***Preserve It Naturally*, Excalibur/KBI Inc**
A very good compendium of tips and tricks to make you a wizard with your kitchen dehydrator.

***Trail Food*, Alan Kesselheim, Ragged Mountain Press**
This little classic is an excellent reference for those desiring to master the art of drying foods for any outdoor excursion.

Informational Websites

American Hiking Society
www.americanhiking.org
The mission of the American Hiking Society is to be the national voice of those who use and love this country's foot trails. The AHS champions conservation issues, builds partnerships, and provides resources to plan, fund, and develop foot trails. Go to their website to find out more about the work of the AHS and the local organizations whose efforts preserve and protect the trails in your neck of the woods.

Backpack Gear Test
www.backpackgeartest.com
Contemplating the purchase of expensive equipment? This is the place to go to see thorough, unbiased reviews of the performance of gear in the field.

Backpacking Light
www.backpackinglight.com
A very good reference for those who want to learn more about how to safely reduce that heavy load on their back.

Epicurious
www.epicurious.com
You won't find much on trail cooking at Epicurious. But if you're looking

to hone your basic cooking skills and could use thousands of recipes for practice, this is a good resource.

Exploratorium

www.exploratorium.edu/cooking

Exploratorium makes cooking fun by putting emphasis on the science behind it. Even if you're not the scientist type, you'll enjoy this site. Quirky yet practical, recipes flow down the page with relevant science posted in the sidebar.

Gourmet Sleuth

www.gourmetsleuth.com

A good kitchen measurement conversion calculator can be found at this website. Included are conversions between United States and British measurement units.

Leave No Trace (LNT) Center for Outdoor Ethics

www.LNT.org

The Center for Outdoor Ethics has been a leader and respected voice in communicating why and how our outdoor places require responsible stewardship. The LNT outdoor ethics code is becoming standard practice within Scouting. More information about the organization is available at their website, and specific information about outdoor ethics principles, especially as applied to cooking, can be found in Appendix D of this book.

Philmont Scout Ranch

www.scouting.org/philmont

A Scout grows through the ranks hearing often of Philmont, BSA's premier high-adventure base for backpacking. Located in the Rockies of New Mexico, Philmont is the apex of the Scouting experience for many and carries a mystique all its own. Follow the web link above to understand why.

Appendix D

LOW-IMPACT COOKING

"Leave a place better than you found it." A Scout hears that phrase innumerable times over the years. In fact, low-impact wilderness ethics has become a core principle within Scouting, the mastery of which is a requirement for rank advancement.

Early Scoutcraft emphasized skills for adapting the camp environment to suit the needs of the outdoorsman. But in more recent years, with increasing use and pressure on our wild places, the emphasis has rightly shifted toward developing wilderness skills within the context of minimizing one's impact on the outdoors and others.

In fact, the Boy Scout Outdoor Code states:

As an American, I will do my best to
Be clean in my outdoor manners
Be careful with fire
Be considerate in the outdoors
Be conservation-minded

By conscientiously following the Scout Outdoor Code, we become better and more thoughtful stewards of our natural resources.

The Leave No Trace Center for Outdoor Ethics also provides a set of principles that are becoming increasingly well known and applied within Scouting. These align closely with the Scout Outdoor Code. The principles of outdoor ethics from Leave No Trace enhance those of the Scout Outdoor Code by providing additional detail on their application.

The seven core principles of Leave No Trace are:

1. Plan ahead and prepare
2. Travel and camp on durable surfaces
3. Dispose of waste properly
4. Leave what you find
5. Minimize campfire impacts
6. Respect wildlife
7. Be considerate of other visitors

Careful planning, especially with respect to food preparation, is critical to successfully following the principles of both the Scout Outdoor Code and Leave No Trace, all of which are touched on once on the trail. When preparing for an upcoming outing, consider the following list of application points as you discuss food and cooking options with your fellow Scouts and Scouters.

Decide how you'll prepare your food.

Some methods of cooking, such as the use of pack stoves, create less impact than others, such as open fires. When using open fire to cook, follow local fire restrictions and use an established fire ring instead of creating a new one. Keep fires small. Collect wood from the ground rather than from standing trees. To avoid creating barren earth, find wood farther away from camp. Select smaller pieces of wood, and burn them completely to ash. Afterward, be sure the fire is completely out, then scatter the ashes. Learn how to use a mound fire to prevent scorching the ground and blackening rocks.

Carefully select and repackage your food to minimize trash.

Tiny pieces of trash easily become litter. Avoid bringing small, individually packaged candies and other such food items on the trail. Twist ties and bread clips are easily lost when dropped. Remove the wrappers and repackage such foods into ziplock bags before leaving home; or use knots, instead of ties and clips, to seal bags and the like.

Metal containers and their lids, crushed beverage cans, and broken glass can easily cut or puncture trash sacks. Wrap them carefully before placing them in thin-wall trash bags. Minimize the use of glass on the trail. Scan your trail camp carefully when packing up to ensure that no litter is left behind.

Minimize leftovers and dispose of food waste properly.

Leftover food makes for messier trash and cleanup. If poured on open ground, it is unsightly and unsanitary. If buried too close to the surface, animals may dig it up. Leftovers encourage problem animals if not properly managed. Carefully plan your meals to reduce leftovers.

These prints were found along a section of the Pacific Crest Trail in an area supposedly lacking bear activity. Never assume an area to be free of nosy critters, and protect your food accordingly. *TIM CONNERS*

Dispose of used wash and rinse water (also called gray water) in a manner appropriate for your area. Before disposal, remove or strain food chunks from the gray water and place these with the trash. Dispose of gray water in a cat hole covered by several inches of soil in an area free of sensitive vegetation and at least 200 feet from streams and lakes. Avoid excessive sudsing by using only the amount of detergent necessary for the job. Bring only biodegradable soap on the trail.

Plan to protect your food, trash, and other odorous items from animals.

Consider avoiding the use of very aromatic foods that can attract animals. Store food, trash, and other odorous items where animals won't be able to get to them. Besides being potentially dangerous to the animal, and inconvenient for the backpacker, trash is often spread over a large area once the animal gains access. Follow local regulations regarding proper food storage, such as the use of bear-bagging techniques or bear-proof food canisters.

While resting unsupervised against a tree below Half Dome in Yosemite National Park, this pack was ruined by a chipmunk that badly wanted the gorp in a side-pocket. Never underestimate the determination and destructive power of wildlife. *TIM CONNERS*

Decide whether to avoid collecting wild foods.

Don't harvest wild foods, such as berries, if these are not plentiful in the area you're visiting. Such foods are likely to be a more important component of the local ecosystem when scarce.

These are only a few of the practical considerations and potential applications of the principles of the Scout Outdoor Code and Leave No Trace. Visit www.LNT.org for additional information and ideas.

These unripe blackberries were found in abundance on the flanks of Blood Mountain on the Appalachian Trail. When berries are scarce, leave them for the wildlife that relies on them for food. *TIM CONNERS*

Appendix E

RELATED RANK AND MERIT BADGE REQUIREMENTS

The following list summarizes all current Boy Scout merit badge requirements related to food preparation that can be accomplished by using the instructional material and recipes in *The Scout's Backpacking Cookbook.*

Keep in mind that rank and merit badge requirements are updated by BSA on a regular basis, and the identification numbers and details for these may change from those shown here. Regardless, the list will point you in the right direction and give a good picture of how this book can be used to satisfy the requirements specific to a given rank or badge.

Rank Advancement

Tenderfoot

3 Assist with preparing and cooking a meal for your patrol on a campout.

Second Class

2(e) Discuss when it is appropriate to use a lightweight stove. Discuss safety procedures when using a lightweight stove.

2(f) Demonstrate how to start a lightweight stove.

First Class

4(a) Help plan a patrol menu consisting of at least one breakfast, one lunch, and one dinner, two meals of which must be cooked.

4(b) Make a list showing the food amounts required to feed three or more boys and secure the ingredients.

4(c) Describe which pans, utensils, and other gear are required to cook and serve these meals.

4(d) Explain the procedures to follow in the safe handling and storage of perishable food products. Tell how to properly dispose of rubbish.

4(e) On a campout, serve as patrol cook and supervise an assistant in using a stove. Prepare the meals from 4(a). Supervise cleanup.

Merit Badges

Backpacking

2(b) Describe ten ways to limit the weight and bulk of items in your backpack without jeopardizing your health or safety.

3(c) Explain how risk can be minimized on a backpacking trip.

4(a) Describe the importance of applying Leave No Trace principles while backpacking and at least five ways to lessen your impact on the environment while on the trail.

4(b) Describe proper methods for handling waste while on a backpacking trip.

5(b) Explain why it is important to stay properly hydrated on a trek.

8(a) Explain the advantages and disadvantages of three different types of backpacking stoves using at least three different kinds of fuel.

8(b) Demonstrate how to safely operate a backpacking stove. Also demonstrate how to handle liquid fuel safely.

8(c) Prepare at least three meals using a stove and fuel that can be carried in a backpack.

8(d) Show how to keep cooking and eating gear clean and sanitary. Demonstrate proper methods for food storage while backpacking.

9(b) Demonstrate how to properly pack your share of the crew's food and gear.

11(a) Develop a list of food and equipment required for a five-day backpacking trip.

11(b) Take the backpacking trip planned in 11(a).

Camping (required for Eagle rank)

2 Learn and explain the Leave No Trace principles and Scout Outdoor Code. Plan how to put these into practice on your next outing.

4(b) Assist a Scout patrol or Webelos unit with menu planning for a campout.

6(b) Discuss the importance of camp sanitation and why water treatment is essential.

7(a) Make a checklist of patrol gear required for your campout.

8(b) Discuss advantages and disadvantages of different types of lightweight stoves.

8(c) Discuss how to protect your food against bad weather, animals, and contamination.

8(d) Cook at least one trail meal using a lightweight stove.

10 Discuss how working through the requirements for this merit badge has taught you about personal health and safety, public health, and conservation.

Cooking

1(a) Describe the injuries that can arise while cooking.

1(b) Explain how perishable foods should be stored, transported, and prepared for cooking.

3(a) Plan a menu for two straight days of camping (six meals total, consisting of two breakfasts, two lunches, and two dinners).

3(b) The menu in 3(a) must include a one-pot dinner, not prepared with canned goods.

3(c) Make a list for the menu from 3(a) showing the food amounts required to feed three or more boys.

3(d) List the utensils required to prepare and serve the meals in 3(a).

4(a) Using the menu from 3(a), prepare for yourself and two others the two dinners, one of either lunch, and one of either breakfast. Time the cooking so that each course will be ready to serve at the proper time. The meals may be prepared during separate trips.

4(b) For meals prepared in requirement 4(a) for which flame is needed, use a backpacking stove to cook at least one meal.

4(c) For each meal in 4(a), use safe food-handling practices. Following each meal, properly dispose of all rubbish by packing out. Clean the cooking area thoroughly.

5(a) Plan a trail menu for one day (three meals) or two days (four meals). The food items should be lightweight and not require refrigeration.

5(b) Make a list for the menu from 5(a) showing the food amounts required to feed three or more boys.

5(c) List the utensils required to prepare and serve the meals in 5(a).

5(d) Determine the weight of the foods in 5(a).

6(a) Using the menu from 5(a), prepare for yourself and two others the trail breakfast and dinner. Time the cooking so that each course will be ready to

Bread baked in a pack oven. *CHRISTINE CONNERS*

serve at the proper time. The meals may be prepared during separate trips.

6(b) Use a backpacking stove under proper supervision for the meals to be prepared in requirement 6(a).

6(c) For each meal in 6(a), use safe food-handling practices. Following each meal, properly dispose of all rubbish by packing out. Clean the cooking area thoroughly.

Fire Safety

10(b) Demonstrate setting up and putting out a cooking fire.

10(d) Explain how to set up a campsite safe from fire.

Fishing

9 Cook a fish that you have caught.

Fly Fishing

10 Cook a fish that you have caught.

Discuss with your Merit Badge Counselor how to best apply this book for the specific rank and merit badges you are working toward.

Appendix F

THE NATIONAL SCENIC TRAILS SYSTEM

Looking for some of most challenging, beautiful, and inspiring places to apply your Scouting skills? Perhaps you've been to Philmont and had a taste of the spectacular majesty of the mountains and are now contemplating where to go next for more? If this is you, then look no further than the National Scenic Trails System.

Created by an Act of Congress to protect corridors of high scenic value, the National Trails System comprises a masterwork of eleven long footpaths distributed across the United States. Each of these trails is an unparalleled scenic gem. Now spanning more than 18,000 trail miles, they were created to provide ultimate access to the country's most awesome wild places. Each trail presents a challenge like no other.

The following list contains basic information about each of the trails, including length and location. You will probably recognize some of the names. In fact, your troop or crew may have walked at least a portion of one of these trails in the past. But were you aware of the others? Did you realize just how truly massive this network of long trails is? The opportunities for exploring are nearly endless.

The National Park Service maintains ultimate oversight of the National Scenic Trails System. But day-to-day trail stewardship is accomplished through volunteer organizations that work closely with federal and state government bureaus. These volunteer organizations are often the best source for up-to-date information, and so web links to these have been provided where applicable in the list below. The Partnership for the National Trails System at www.pnts.org is also a good launching point to those organizations directly associated with each of the National Scenic Trails.

And while the National Scenic Trails may be the most famous of the long trails, they are by no means the only ones. Information regarding other backpacking options can be found through the National Park Service at www.nps.gov/nts, the US Forest Service at www.fs.fed.us/recreation/programs/trails, and the Bureau of Land Management at www.blm.gov.

So keep on challenging yourself. Browse the following list, follow the web links to learn more about our incredible long trails, and be inspired.

Appalachian

2,174 miles, Georgia to Maine

Information: Appalachian Trail Conservancy at www.appalachiantrail.org

Arizona

807 miles, Mexico-Arizona border to Utah-Arizona border

Information: Arizona Trail Association at www.aztrail.org

Continental Divide

3,100 miles, Mexico-New Mexico border to Canada-Montana border

Information: Continental Divide Trail Alliance at www.cdtrail.org

Florida

1,400 miles, entirely within the state of Florida

Information: Florida Trail Association at www.floridatrail.org

Ice Age

1,200 miles, entirely within the state of Wisconsin

Information: Ice Age Trail Alliance at www.iceagetrail.org

Natchez Trace

65 miles, four segments in Mississippi and Tennessee

Information: National Park Service at www.nps.gov/natt/index.htm

New England
220 miles, Connecticut to Massachusetts
Information: Connecticut Forest and Park Association and Appalachian Mountain Club at www.newenglandnst.org

North Country
4,600 miles, New York to North Dakota
Information: North Country Trail Association at www.northcountrytrail.org

Pacific Crest
2,638 miles, Mexico-California border to Canada-Washington border
Information: Pacific Crest Trail Association at www.pcta.org

Pacific Northwest
1,200 miles, Montana to Washington
Information: Pacific Northwest Trail Association at www.pnt.org

Potomac Heritage
830 miles, Virginia to Pennsylvania
Information: Potomac Heritage Trail Association at www.potomactrail.org

Index

About the Authors

Experienced backpackers, campers, and outdoor chefs, Tim and Christine Conners are the authors of the popular trail cookbooks *Lipsmackin' Backpackin'* and *Lipsmackin' Vegetarian Backpackin'*. Specifically for the Scouting world, they've also authored *The Scout's Outdoor Cookbook, The Scout's Dutch Oven Cookbook,* and *The Scout's Large Groups Cookbook,* each a collection of unique and outstanding camp recipes from Scout leaders across the United States.

Tim and Christine have been testing outdoor recipes for over fifteen years now. At the invitation of Boy Scouts of America, the Conners have twice served as judges for *Scouting* magazine's prestigious national camp food cooking contest.

The Conners have four children, James, Michael, Maria, and David, their youngest. Tim is Assistant Scoutmaster and Christine is Committee Member and Merit Badge Counselor for the Coastal Empire Council's Troop 340 in Statesboro, Georgia, where their two oldest sons have attained the rank of Life Scout and are on the road to Eagle.

The Conners family stays busy in the outdoors by backpacking on the Appalachian Trail, camping and day-hiking in the local state parks, and kayaking on the region's lakes and rivers . . . when they aren't writing cookbooks.

Stop by www.scoutcooking.com to say howdy!

The Conners family sharing dinner on the Appalachian Trail. DAVID LATTNER